Mastering Customer Support

Book 4

8 Books to 8 Figures Series

Jason Miller

Copyright 2024 Jason Miller

ALL RIGHTS RESERVED. This book contains material protected under International and Federal Copyright Laws and Treaties. Any unauthorized reprint or use of this material is prohibited. No part of this book may be reproduced or transmitted in any form or by any means, electronic or mechanical, including photocopying, recording, or by any information storage and retrieval system, without express written permission from the author/publisher.

ISBN: 978-1-957217-49-9 (hardcover)
ISBN: 978-1-957217-48-2 (paperback)
ISBN: 978-1-957217-50-5 (ebook)

TABLE OF CONTENTS

Introduction: The Power of Customer Contact......... v

Chapter 1: Feedback Loops and Continuous
            Improvement....................... 1

Chapter 2: Training and Development for
            Support Staff....................... 10

Chapter 3: Multichannel Support Strategies......... 27

Chapter 4: Measuring Customer Support Success..... 46

Chapter 5: Building a Customer-Centric Culture..... 62

Chapter 6: Implementing Effective Customer
            Feedback Systems.................... 80

Chapter 7: Leveraging Technology for
            Multichannel Support 98

Conclusion: The Path to Exceptional
            Customer Support.................. 117

INTRODUCTION: THE POWER OF CUSTOMER CONTACT

Customer contact is the heartbeat of any successful business. It's where the magic happens—the moment when a customer reaches out, seeking help, guidance, or reassurance. This initial interaction is an opportunity to build trust, foster loyalty, and leave a lasting impression.

As a business owner, I've come to understand the critical importance of customer contact firsthand. It's not just about addressing a query or solving a problem; it's about making a connection, showing empathy, and delivering an experience that exceeds expectations.

The unwavering commitment to providing exceptional customer service is at the core of it all. This overarching theme guides every interaction, every decision, and every initiative within my business. Because I know that in today's competitive landscape, it's not enough to meet customer needs—we must strive to surpass them at every turn.

Customer contact sets the stage for the entire support process. It's the initial point of contact where trust is either established or eroded. That's why I prioritize it above all else, recognizing it as the foundation for lasting relationships.

In the following pages, we'll explore the nuances of customer contact and delve deeper into the strategies and techniques that can elevate it from a mere transaction to a memorable experience. However, before we embark on this journey, it's essential to grasp the pivotal role that customer contact plays in shaping the customer experience and, ultimately, the success of our businesses.

Reflecting on my experiences as a business owner, I can't help but emphasize the profound impact that exceptional customer support encounters have on shaping perceptions of a brand. These interactions are not just transactions; they're opportunities to create meaningful connections and leave lasting impressions.

When customers encounter exceptional support, it's like a breath of fresh air—a reassuring sign that their needs are valued and their concerns will be addressed. These positive interactions go beyond resolving immediate issues; they foster a sense of trust and confidence in the brand. Customers feel heard, understood, and appreciated, strengthening their loyalty and commitment to the company.

Moreover, positive interactions contribute significantly to customer satisfaction. When customers receive prompt, empathetic, and effective support, it enhances their overall experience with the brand. They're more likely to become repeat customers and advocates, spreading positive word-of-mouth and driving new business.

On the other hand, negative support encounters can have detrimental effects on a brand's reputation. When customers feel ignored, dismissed, or mistreated, it erodes trust and undermines their confidence in the company. They may share their negative experiences with others, tarnishing the brand's image and potentially deterring future customers.

I've come to appreciate the immense value of prioritizing exemplary customer support. It's not just about addressing problems but building relationships and fostering loyalty. By investing in training, empowering support teams, and consistently delivering exceptional service, I can ensure that every customer interaction contributes positively to our brand's reputation and success.

As we embark on this journey together, I want to give you a sneak peek into what lies ahead in this book. We will explore some crucial themes and dive into practical strategies that can transform how you approach customer support in your business.

First, we'll discuss the importance of feedback loops and continuous improvement. We'll explore how gathering feedback from customers post-interaction can drive ongoing enhancements in service quality. From surveys to social media monitoring, we'll uncover various methods for collecting valuable insights that can help you fine-tune your support processes.

Next, we'll delve into the world of training and development for support staff. We'll cover topics like empathy training, technical skill enhancement, and stress management, equipping your team with the tools they need to handle a wide range of customer interactions effectively.

Then, we'll tackle the challenge of multichannel support strategies. In today's digital age, offering support across multiple channels like phone, email, social media, and live chat is essential. We'll discuss how to maintain consistency and quality across these platforms and tailor the customer experience for each channel.

After that, we'll shift our focus to measuring customer support success. We'll introduce metrics and key performance indicators essential for evaluating the effectiveness of your support efforts. From first response time to customer satisfaction scores, we'll explore the metrics that matter most and how to use them to drive improvement.

Finally, we'll explore the importance of building a customer-centric culture within your organization. We'll discuss how fostering a culture that prioritizes customer needs and values can enhance the overall effectiveness of your support efforts. From leadership's role in setting customer-focused values to fostering behaviors that prioritize customer satisfaction, we'll uncover the secrets to creating a culture that puts the customer first.

Throughout these chapters, you can expect to gain valuable insights and actionable strategies you can implement in your business immediately. Get ready to revolutionize your approach to customer support and take your business to new heights.

Now that we've laid the groundwork and explored the key themes of customer support, it's time to take action. I want to encourage you to embark on a journey with me to master the art of customer support and elevate your business success to new heights.

In the following chapters, we'll dive deep into the strategies and techniques that can help you harness the power of customer contact effectively. Whether you're a seasoned entrepreneur or just starting out, there's something valuable to be gained from each chapter.

I invite you to grab a copy of this book and join me on this adventure. Together, we'll learn how to gather feedback, train and develop support staff, implement multichannel support strategies, measure success, and build a customer-centric culture.

You'll be better equipped to exceed customer expectations, foster loyalty, and drive growth by mastering and applying these skills in your business. Let's roll up our sleeves and get started. Your journey to mastering customer support begins now.

1

FEEDBACK LOOPS AND CONTINUOUS IMPROVEMENT

INTRODUCTION TO FEEDBACK LOOPS

In the world of business, feedback is like the compass that guides us toward success. Think of it as a continuous loop—a cycle of information flowing back and forth between us and our customers. This concept is what we call feedback loops.

What exactly are feedback loops? Well, they're quite simple. After every interaction with a customer, whether a phone call, an email, or a chat session, we gather feedback. This feedback could be in the form of a survey response, a comment on social media, or even a direct message from a customer.

You might be wondering why gathering feedback is so important. Let me break it down for you. Feedback is like a window into the minds of our customers. It gives us valuable insight into what they liked and didn't like and what we can do better next time. Without feedback, we're just shooting in the dark, hoping we're on the right track.

However, feedback loops aren't just about collecting feedback for the sake of it. They're about using that feedback to drive continuous improvement in the quality of our service.

It's like a never-ending cycle of learning and adapting based on the needs and preferences of our customers.

By listening to our customers and making changes based on their feedback, we're able to meet and exceed their expectations. And that's what sets apart businesses that thrive from those that merely survive. So, buckle up because we're about to embark on a journey to master the art of feedback loops and take our customer support to the next level.

Methods for Collecting Feedback

When it comes to gathering feedback from our customers, there's no shortage of methods to choose from. We have surveys, social media monitoring, and direct outreach—each with its own set of pros and cons.

Let's start with surveys. Surveys are like digital comment cards we can send our customers to get their thoughts and opinions. They're great because they allow us to collect a lot of feedback from many people in a relatively short amount of time. Plus, they're easy to analyze and quantify. However, surveys also have their limitations. Sometimes, customers might not be inclined to fill them out, or they might not accurately represent the views of our entire customer base.

Then, there's social media monitoring. With social media, we can keep an eye on what people are saying about us online—whether it's on Twitter, Facebook, or any other platform. This gives us real-time insight into how our customers feel and allows us to respond quickly to any issues or concerns. However, social media monitoring can be time-consuming, and not all customers will voice their opinions publicly.

Lastly, there's direct customer outreach. This could involve things like phone calls, emails, or one-on-one meetings with customers. Direct outreach allows us to have more personal conversations with our customers and get detailed feedback tailored to their specific experiences. The downside is that it can be resource-intensive and might not always be feasible for every customer.

Let me give you a real-life example of how we've used these feedback collection methods in my own business. Last year, we launched a new product line, and to gauge customer satisfaction, we sent out a survey to everyone who made a purchase. We also monitored social media channels for any mentions of the new products and reached out to select customers for in-depth interviews. This multi-pronged approach allowed us to gather comprehensive feedback and improve based on what our customers told us.

As you can see, there's no one-size-fits-all approach to collecting feedback. It's all about finding the right mix of methods for our business and customers.

Importance of Analyzing Feedback

Understanding feedback is like having a treasure map for improving our business. It's not just about collecting feedback; it's about what we do with it that counts.

When we gather customer feedback, we get a glimpse into their thoughts and feelings about our products or services. However, it's not enough to just collect that feedback—we need to dig deeper and analyze it to uncover insights that can help us make informed decisions.

One technique we can use is sentiment analysis. This involves looking at the language and tone of the feedback to determine whether it's positive, negative, or neutral. By understanding the sentiment behind the feedback, we can identify areas where we're excelling and areas where we might need to improve.

Another technique is categorization. This involves organizing feedback into different categories based on common themes or topics. For example, we might categorize feedback related to pricing, customer service, product quality, and so on. This allows us to see patterns and trends across different areas of our business.

Here is an example of how feedback analysis can drive improvements. Let's say we've been receiving a lot of negative feedback about our customer service response times. By analyzing this feedback, we discover that customers are frustrated with long wait times when they call in for support. Armed with this insight, we can take action to improve our response times, whether it's by hiring more support staff, implementing better technology, or providing additional training.

Ultimately, feedback analysis isn't just about looking at numbers and charts—it's about using that information to make meaningful changes that benefit our customers and our business. It's about turning feedback into action and continuously striving to deliver the best possible experience for our customers.

Implementing Actionable Changes

Implementing actionable changes based on customer feedback is like steering a ship in the right direction. It's not enough to just know where we need to improve; we have to chart a course and set sail.

One strategy for translating feedback into action is prioritizing initiatives based on their impact and feasibility. We can't tackle everything at once, so focusing on the changes that will impact our customers and business the most is important. For example, if we receive consistent feedback about a specific product issue, addressing that issue should take precedence over less pressing matters.

Allocating resources effectively is also key. This means ensuring we have the right people, time, and budget to support our feedback-driven initiatives. It might involve reallocating resources from less critical projects or investing in new tools and technologies to support our efforts.

Let me share a case study to illustrate how this works in practice. Imagine we're a software company, and we've been getting feedback from our users about a product bug causing frustration and delays. Instead of ignoring this feedback or putting it on the back burner, we prioritize it as a high-impact issue and allocate resources to fix it quickly. We assemble a team of developers, testers, and support staff to address the issue, and within a few weeks, we release a patch that resolves the bug. As a result, our customers are happier, our support team is less overwhelmed, and our business reputation is strengthened.

By taking a systematic approach to implementing feedback-driven changes, we can ensure that our efforts are focused where they matter most and that we're making meaningful improvements that benefit both our customers and our business. It's about being proactive, strategic, and responsive to our customers' needs— ultimately, that's what sets successful businesses apart.

Monitoring and Iterating

In the world of business, nothing stays the same for long. That's why it's crucial to understand that improving customer support isn't a one-and-done deal—it's an ongoing journey of monitoring, adjusting, and fine-tuning.

Think of it like tuning a guitar. You don't just pluck the strings once and expect them to stay perfectly in tune forever. You must keep adjusting, listening, and tweaking until you find that sweet spot.

The same goes for customer support. Our job isn't finished once we've implemented changes based on feedback. We must keep a close eye on how those changes work in the real world.

Are customers happier? Are support issues being resolved more quickly? Are our teams more efficient?

By regularly monitoring and evaluating our customer support efforts, we can identify areas where we're excelling and areas where we still need to improve. Maybe the fix we implemented for that product bug worked great, but now we're noticing a different issue cropping up more frequently. Or maybe our response times have improved, but our customer satisfaction scores haven't budged.

That's where iteration comes in. It's about taking what we've learned from our monitoring efforts and using that insight to make targeted adjustments to our processes. Maybe we need to tweak our support workflows, update our training materials, or invest in new technology to address emerging needs.

One effective technique for iterating is to set up regular feedback loops with our teams and customers. This could involve regular check-ins, surveys, or focus groups to gather insights and ideas for improvement. By keeping the lines of communication open and actively seeking input, we can ensure that we're always evolving and adapting to meet the changing needs of our customers.

Ultimately, monitoring and iterating are about staying agile and responsive in a fast-paced business environment. It's about never being satisfied with the status quo and always striving to deliver the best possible experience for our customers. Because when we're constantly listening, learning, and improving, there's no limit to how far we can go.

Leveraging Technology for Feedback Management

In today's digital age, technology is a must-have for businesses looking to stay competitive. And when it comes to managing feedback, technology can be a game-changer.

There's a whole world of tools and platforms out there designed to make feedback collection and analysis easier and more efficient. The options are endless, from simple survey tools to robust customer feedback management systems.

One tool that's become increasingly popular is the customer feedback management system. These platforms are like command centers for your feedback efforts, allowing you to collect, analyze, and act on customer feedback all in one place. They can automatically gather feedback from multiple channels—like email, social media, and chat—and aggregate it into actionable insights.

However, with so many options to choose from, how do you know which technology solution is right for your business? It all comes down to your specific needs and priorities. Are you looking for a simple, plug-and-play solution, or do you need something more customizable and scalable? Do you have a large team that needs access to feedback data, or are you flying solo?

When selecting a technology solution, it's important to do your homework. Take the time to research different options, read reviews, and maybe even test-drive a few platforms to see which one feels like the best fit for your business.

Once you've chosen a technology solution, the next step is implementation. This is where many businesses stumble. But fear not—implementing a new technology solution can be a breeze with the right approach. Start by setting clear goals and objectives for what you want to achieve with the new system. Then, make sure you have buy-in from key stakeholders and provide thorough training for your team.

With the right technology in place, managing feedback becomes not just easier but also more effective. You'll have the tools you need to collect, analyze, and act on feedback in real time, helping you stay ahead of the curve and deliver an exceptional customer experience every step of the way.

CREATING A FEEDBACK-FOCUSED CULTURE

Creating a culture that puts customer feedback front and center is crucial for any business looking to thrive in today's competitive landscape. When customers feel their voices are heard and their opinions matter, they're more likely to stick around and keep returning for more.

However, fostering this kind of feedback-focused culture isn't always easy. It takes time, effort, and a whole lot of commitment from everyone involved. That means not just me as the business owner but also my team members and even our customers themselves.

One strategy that's worked well for us is to make giving feedback as easy and convenient as possible. We've set up multiple channels for customers to share their thoughts, whether it's through surveys, social media, or good old-fashioned email. And we've made sure to let them know that their feedback is not just welcome but actively encouraged.

However, it's not just about collecting feedback—it's also about acting on it. That means taking the time to review and analyze the feedback we receive and then using it to make real, meaningful changes to our products, services, and processes. It's a continuous cycle of listening, learning, and improving.

Of course, none of this would be possible without strong leadership. As the captain of the ship, it's my job to set the tone and lead by example when it comes to valuing and prioritizing customer feedback. That means being open to criticism, admitting when we've made mistakes, and always striving to do better.

Perhaps most importantly, it means empowering my team members to take ownership of the feedback process themselves. After all, they're the ones on the front lines, interacting with customers daily. By giving them the tools and support they need to gather and act on feedback effectively, I'm not just building a feedback-focused culture—I'm building a stronger, more customer-centric business from the ground up.

Conclusion: The Power of Feedback Loops

As I wrap up this chapter on the power of feedback loops, I can't help but reflect on the valuable insights we've covered. We've talked about how crucial it is to gather customer feedback, whether through surveys, social media, or direct conversations. We've also explored how analyzing this feedback can help us make smarter, more informed decisions about improving our products and services.

Perhaps most importantly, we've seen how feedback loops aren't just a one-time thing but an ongoing process. It's not enough to collect feedback once and call it a day. Instead, we need to constantly monitor, analyze, and iterate based on the feedback we receive. It's a cycle of continuous improvement that never ends.

As I've said before, feedback is a gift. It's a chance for us to learn and grow, to become better versions of ourselves and better businesses for our customers. So my call to action for you, dear reader, is simple: prioritize feedback. Make it a central part of your organization's culture. And most importantly, use it to drive real, meaningful change in your business.

At the end of the day, it's not just about collecting feedback—it's about using it to make a difference. By harnessing the power of feedback loops, I truly believe that we can all take our businesses to new heights of success.

2
TRAINING AND DEVELOPMENT FOR SUPPORT STAFF

Training and development are the backbone of any successful customer support team. It's about making sure my staff has the skills they need to handle any situation that comes their way when they're helping our customers. When I say training and development, I mean giving them the tools and knowledge to do their job better every day. Whether it's learning how to use our support systems more efficiently or honing their communication skills, it's all about helping them grow professionally.

In our company, training and development mean investing in our people so they can deliver top-notch service. It's not just about teaching them how to answer calls or respond to emails—it's about empowering them to solve problems and make our customers happy. So, when I talk about training and development, I'm talking about giving our team the resources they need to succeed and thrive in their roles. That's what sets us apart and keeps our customers coming back.

Investing in the growth and development of my support staff is crucial for the success of our business. When my team members feel supported and equipped with the right skills, they're better able to handle any challenges that come their way when assisting our customers. That's why I prioritize continuous learning and growth within our support team.

In this chapter, we'll dive into strategies to enhance our support teams' skills and capabilities. From communication skills to technical knowledge, there's always room for improvement, and I'm committed to providing my team with the tools they need to succeed. By focusing on their development, we can ensure they're equipped to provide top-notch service to our customers, ultimately driving satisfaction and loyalty.

Throughout this chapter, we'll explore various strategies and techniques to empower our support staff to excel in their roles. Because when they thrive, our business thrives, too.

Understanding the Importance of Training

As a business owner, I've come to understand the critical role that training plays in the success of our support staff. Training isn't just about teaching employees how to perform specific tasks; it's about equipping them with the knowledge and skills they need to excel in their roles and provide exceptional service to our customers.

When our support staff undergoes thorough training, they gain a deeper understanding of our products or services, our company values, and the best practices for interacting with customers. This builds their confidence and enhances their ability to effectively address customer inquiries, troubleshoot issues, and provide solutions.

Moreover, training fosters a culture of continuous improvement within our team. Investing in ongoing training opportunities demonstrates our commitment to supporting our staff's professional growth and development. This, in turn, boosts morale and motivation, leading to higher levels of job satisfaction and employee retention.

Training is the foundation upon which our support team's success is built. It sets the stage for them to deliver outstanding service, uphold our company's reputation, and ultimately contribute to our business's overall growth and prosperity.

Having a well-trained staff is like having a secret weapon in the business world. It's not just about having employees who know how to do their jobs; it's about having a team that can knock customer service out of the park. When our staff is trained to the highest standards, it makes a world of difference in how our customers feel about our company.

Let me give you an example. Last year, we implemented a comprehensive training program for our support team. We covered everything from product knowledge to communication skills. And you know what? The results were incredible. Our customer satisfaction scores shot through the roof, and we saw a significant increase in customer loyalty.

One of my favorite stories from that time was when a customer called in with a complex issue. Instead of being passed around or put on hold, they were connected with a support agent who had been through our training program. Not only did they solve the problem quickly and efficiently, but they also took the time to explain everything in a way that the customer could understand. The customer was so impressed that they wrote us a glowing review online and even referred their friends to us.

That's the power of well-trained staff. They don't just provide solutions; they create memorable experiences that keep customers coming back for more. And in today's competitive business landscape, that kind of loyalty is priceless.

Designing Effective Training Programs

When it comes to training our support staff, I've learned that one size definitely doesn't fit all. Each member of our team has different strengths, weaknesses, and learning styles, so it's crucial to design training programs that cater to their individual needs.

One strategy we've found effective is to start by identifying the specific skills and knowledge gaps within our support team. We do this through a combination of performance evaluations, feedback from team members, and observations of their interactions with customers. By pinpointing areas where our team could use extra support, we can tailor our training programs to address those needs.

Another key aspect of designing effective training programs is to make them as interactive and engaging as possible. We've found that hands-on activities, role-playing exercises, and real-world scenarios are much more effective than simply lecturing our team members. Not only does this approach keep them actively engaged in the learning process, but it also gives them the opportunity to practice their new skills in a safe environment.

Ensuring that our training programs are flexible and adaptable is also essential. As our business evolves and our customer needs change, so too must our training programs. We regularly review and update our training materials to ensure that they remain relevant and effective.

By taking a personalized, interactive, and flexible approach to designing our training programs, we've empowered our support staff to excel in their roles and deliver exceptional service to our customers. And that's what it's all about at the end of the day – providing our team with the tools and knowledge they need to succeed.

When it comes to training our support staff, I've found that incorporating various learning methods is key to keeping things fresh and engaging. We mix things up with workshops, simulations, and online courses to cater to different learning styles and preferences.

Workshops are great for bringing the team together in a collaborative environment. We can cover a lot of ground in a short amount of time and encourage active participation through discussions and group activities. It's a hands-on approach that allows our staff to learn from each other's experiences and perspectives.

Simulations take things a step further by putting our team members in realistic scenarios where they can practice their skills in a safe, controlled environment. Whether it's dealing with a difficult customer or troubleshooting a complex issue, simulations give our staff the opportunity to apply what they've learned and refine their techniques.

Online courses offer flexibility and convenience, allowing our team members to learn at their own pace and on their own schedule. We provide access to a variety of courses covering everything from technical skills to customer service best practices. This way, our staff can continue their development outside of the office and tailor their learning to their specific interests and needs.

Regardless of the learning method, setting clear objectives and outcomes for our training initiatives is crucial. We need to know what we're aiming to achieve and how we'll measure success. Whether improving response times, increasing customer satisfaction scores, or reducing escalations, having clear goals helps keep our training efforts focused and effective.

By incorporating various learning methods and setting clear objectives, we can provide our support staff with the tools and knowledge they need to excel in their roles. Ultimately, that leads to happier customers and a more successful business.

EMPATHY TRAINING FOR SUPPORT STAFF

Empathy is the secret sauce of exceptional customer support. It's not just about solving problems; it's about understanding how our customers feel and showing them that we care. That's why empathy training is crucial to our support staff's development.

In our training sessions, we dive into the role of empathy in customer interactions. We discuss why putting ourselves in our customers' shoes and seeing things from their perspective is important. After all, empathy is what allows us to connect with our customers on a deeper level and build trust and rapport.

We talk about how we can demonstrate empathy, from active listening techniques to acknowledging our customers' emotions and concerns. It's about making our customers feel heard and valued, even when they're facing challenges or frustrations.

One of the key aspects of empathy training is practicing empathy in real-life scenarios. We role-play common support interactions and focus on responding with empathy and compassion. This hands-on approach helps our staff develop their empathy skills in a safe and supportive environment.

By the end of our empathy training sessions, our support staff walk away with a deeper understanding of the importance of empathy in customer support. They're better equipped to handle difficult situations with grace and empathy, ultimately leading to more positive outcomes for our customers and our business.

Teaching our support staff to empathize with our customers' concerns and emotions is a cornerstone of our training program. It's not just about understanding the technical aspects of our products or services; it's about understanding the people behind the inquiries and issues.

One technique we use is storytelling. We share real-life scenarios where our customers faced challenges or had specific needs, and we ask our staff to imagine themselves in the customers' shoes. This helps them see things from a different perspective and understand the impact of their actions on our customers' experiences.

Another technique is active listening. We emphasize the importance of listening to what our customers are saying, how they're saying it, and what emotions they might be expressing. By tuning into our customers' tone of voice and body language, our staff can better empathize with their concerns and provide more personalized support.

We also encourage our staff to validate our customers' emotions and concerns. Instead of dismissing or downplaying their feelings, we teach our staff to acknowledge and empathize with them. This helps our customers feel understood and valued, which can go a long way in building trust and rapport.

Through case studies, we showcase the benefits of empathy training in action. We share stories of how our staff's empathetic responses turned frustrated customers into loyal advocates. These real-life examples demonstrate the tangible impact of empathy on improving customer relationships and driving business success.

Technical Skill Enhancement

Ensuring that our support staff possesses strong technical skills is vital in providing efficient and effective assistance to our customers. When customers reach out to us with technical issues or questions, they expect prompt and accurate solutions. That's why we place a significant emphasis on enhancing the technical proficiency of our support team.

Having a deep understanding of our products or services allows our support staff to troubleshoot problems more effectively. Whether it's diagnosing software glitches, configuring hardware setups, or navigating complex features, our team needs to be well-versed in all aspects of our offerings.

Furthermore, technical proficiency enables our support staff to provide proactive guidance and advice to customers. Instead of just reacting to issues as they arise, our team can anticipate potential challenges and provide preemptive solutions. This proactive approach not only improves customer satisfaction but also helps prevent future issues from occurring.

In today's digital age, technology is constantly evolving, and new tools and platforms are emerging regularly. Therefore, ongoing training and development are essential to ensure that our support staff stays up to date with the latest advancements in our industry. Investing in continuous learning empowers our team to adapt to changes swiftly and maintain their technical expertise.

Ultimately, technical skill enhancement is not just about resolving immediate issues—it's about empowering our support staff to become trusted advisors to our customers. We position our team to deliver exceptional service and foster long-term customer relationships by equipping them with the knowledge and skills they need to excel.

In our quest to ensure top-notch support for our customers, we're constantly refining our strategies to enhance our team's technical skills. One effective approach we've found is through hands-on training and certifications.

Hands-on training allows our support staff to dive deep into the intricacies of our products or services. Instead of just learning theory, they get practical experience tackling real-world challenges. Whether it's through simulated scenarios or guided exercises, hands-on training equips our team with the practical knowledge they need to excel in their roles.

Additionally, we encourage our support staff to pursue relevant certifications in their areas of expertise. These certifications serve as formal recognition of their skills and knowledge, instilling confidence in both our team members and our customers. By investing in certifications, we're enhancing the credibility of our support staff and signaling our commitment to excellence in customer service.

Staying abreast of evolving technologies and tools is crucial in the fast-paced world of customer support. To achieve this, we foster a culture of continuous learning within our team. We encourage regular participation in workshops, webinars, and industry events to stay updated on the latest trends and developments. Furthermore, we allocate dedicated time for self-study and exploration, allowing our team members to experiment with new tools and technologies relevant to their roles.

Combining hands-on training, certifications, and a commitment to staying current with emerging technologies ensures our support staff remains at the forefront of innovation. This proactive approach not only benefits our team but also translates into enhanced support experiences for our customers.

STRESS MANAGEMENT TECHNIQUES

Navigating the world of customer support can sometimes feel like riding a rollercoaster. As a business owner, I understand the stressful nature of these roles firsthand. Our support team members are on the front lines, dealing with a wide range of customer inquiries, issues, and sometimes even complaints. It's a demanding job that requires technical expertise and emotional resilience.

Recognizing the toll that stress can take on our team members, we prioritize implementing effective stress management techniques. We understand that managing stress isn't just about preventing burnout; it's also about ensuring that our team members can perform at their best and provide exceptional customer support.

One approach we've found valuable is promoting a healthy work-life balance. We encourage our team members to take regular breaks, disconnect from work during non-working hours, and engage in activities that help them recharge. Whether it's spending time with family and friends, pursuing hobbies, or simply enjoying some quiet time alone, we believe that a well-rested and rejuvenated team is better equipped to handle the challenges of customer support.

In addition to promoting work-life balance, we also provide resources and support for managing stress effectively. This includes offering access to counseling services, organizing workshops on stress management techniques, and providing tools for practicing mindfulness and relaxation. By empowering our team members with these resources, we can create a supportive environment where they feel equipped to handle the demands of their roles.

Furthermore, we foster a culture of open communication within our team, where team members feel comfortable discussing their challenges and seeking assistance when needed. This ensures that no one feels overwhelmed or isolated when dealing with stress-related issues.

By acknowledging the stressful nature of customer support roles and proactively implementing stress management techniques, we can support the well-being of our team members and ultimately deliver better outcomes for our customers. After all, a happy and healthy support team is the foundation of exceptional customer service.

As a business owner, one of my top priorities is ensuring the well-being of my support staff. I understand firsthand the pressures and challenges that come with working in customer support roles. Dealing with demanding customers, solving complex issues, and managing a high volume of inquiries can take its toll over time.

That's why I've introduced stress management techniques to help my support staff cope with the pressure and avoid burnout. It's essential for them to feel supported and equipped to handle the demands of their roles effectively.

Firstly, I've emphasized the importance of self-care and work-life balance. I encourage my team members to take regular breaks, disconnect from work outside of their designated hours, and engage in activities that help them relax and recharge. Whether it's spending time with loved ones, pursuing hobbies, or simply enjoying some downtime, prioritizing self-care is crucial for maintaining mental and emotional well-being.

Additionally, I've provided resources and support for practicing stress management techniques. This includes offering access to counseling services, organizing workshops on stress management, and providing tools for practicing mindfulness and relaxation. By empowering my team with these resources, I aim to create a supportive environment where they feel equipped to manage stress effectively.

Communication is also key in addressing stress and preventing burnout. I've fostered a culture of open communication within my team, where team members feel comfortable discussing their challenges and seeking assistance when needed. This ensures that no one feels overwhelmed or isolated in dealing with stress-related issues and encourages a collaborative approach to problem-solving.

Overall, by introducing stress management techniques and prioritizing the well-being of my support staff, I'm committed to creating a positive work environment where they can thrive and continue to deliver exceptional service to our customers. After all, a happy and healthy support team is essential for the success of any business.

In our fast-paced business environment, I understand how crucial it is for my support staff to manage their stress effectively. That's why I've implemented various strategies to help them stay calm, focused, and resilient, even during the busiest of times.

One approach we've embraced is mindfulness practices. I've introduced simple mindfulness exercises that my team can incorporate into their daily routines. These exercises help them stay present and focused, reducing feelings of overwhelm and anxiety. For example, we encourage taking short mindfulness breaks throughout the day to pause, breathe deeply, and refocus their attention. By incorporating mindfulness into their workday, my team has found it easier to stay centered and maintain a positive mindset, even when dealing with challenging customer interactions.

In addition to mindfulness, we've also integrated relaxation exercises into our support team's routine. These exercises help alleviate tension and promote relaxation, making it easier for my team to manage stress effectively. Whether it's practicing deep breathing exercises, progressive muscle relaxation, or guided imagery, these relaxation techniques offer valuable tools for combating stress and promoting overall well-being.

Furthermore, I've emphasized the importance of effective time management strategies. By helping my team prioritize tasks, set realistic goals, and manage their workload efficiently, we can prevent feelings of overwhelm and reduce stress levels. We've implemented techniques such as breaking tasks into smaller, more manageable steps, using time-blocking to schedule dedicated focus periods, and setting boundaries to protect time for important tasks and personal activities.

By implementing mindfulness practices, relaxation exercises, and time management strategies, I'm equipping my support staff with the tools they need to manage stress effectively and thrive in their roles. These practices benefit my team's well-being and contribute to our overall productivity and success as a business.

Role-Playing and Scenario-Based Training

As a business owner, I've found that role-playing and scenario-based training are invaluable tools for preparing my support staff to handle real-world customer interactions effectively. These training methods simulate common support scenarios, allowing team members to practice their communication skills and problem-solving abilities in a safe and controlled environment.

When designing role-playing exercises, I focus on creating realistic scenarios that mirror the challenges my support team may encounter daily. Whether addressing a customer complaint, troubleshooting a technical issue, or diffusing a tense situation, I ensure that the scenarios are relevant and reflective of the types of interactions my team will face.

During these training sessions, I encourage my team members to fully immerse themselves in their roles, playing the part of both the customer and the support representative. This hands-on approach helps them develop empathy and understand the customer's perspective, enabling them to provide more personalized and effective support.

After each role-playing exercise, we hold debriefing sessions where team members receive constructive feedback on their performance. These sessions provide an opportunity for reflection and learning, allowing my team to identify areas for improvement and refine their skills. I help my team members grow and develop their capabilities as support professionals by providing actionable feedback and guidance.

Overall, role-playing and scenario-based training offer numerous benefits for my support team. Not only do they provide practical experience and skill development, but they also foster confidence and readiness when facing real customer interactions. By investing in these training methods, I ensure that my support staff is well-equipped to deliver exceptional service and uphold the reputation of our business.

Continuous Learning and Development

I've always emphasized the importance of continuous learning and development for my support team. I believe that staying ahead in today's fast-paced world means constantly improving our skills and knowledge.

I encourage my support staff to see learning as a lifelong journey, not just something done in the classroom. Whether it's attending workshops, taking online courses, or reading industry articles, there are countless ways to expand our knowledge and grow professionally.

I often remind my team that investing in their development benefits them individually and strengthens our entire support team and our business. By continuously improving our skills and staying updated on industry trends, we can provide better service to our customers and stay competitive in the market.

I provide access to various resources and platforms for self-directed learning and skill enhancement to support their learning journey. From online courses and webinars to industry conferences and networking events, there's something for everyone to explore and learn from.

I also encourage my team to share their newfound knowledge and insights with each other. By fostering a culture of collaboration and knowledge-sharing, we create an environment where everyone can learn from one another and grow together.

Overall, I believe that continuous learning and development are essential for the long-term success of my support team. By embracing a mindset of lifelong learning, we can adapt to changing circumstances, overcome challenges, and achieve our goals.

Leadership's Role in Training and Development

As the leader of my business, I understand the critical role I play in supporting the training and development of my support staff. It's not just about providing resources or scheduling training sessions; it's about actively championing a culture of learning and growth within the team.

One of the key strategies I employ is leading by example. I make it a point to prioritize my learning and development, whether it's attending leadership seminars, taking online courses, or seeking mentorship from industry experts. I inspire my team to do the same by demonstrating my commitment to continuous improvement.

I also believe in providing personalized mentorship to my team members. Each person has unique strengths, weaknesses, and career goals, so I take the time to understand their individual needs and provide guidance and support accordingly. Whether it's offering constructive feedback, facilitating networking opportunities, or recommending relevant learning resources, I strive to empower each team member to reach their full potential.

Another important aspect of leadership's role in training and development is creating a safe and supportive environment where team members feel encouraged to take risks and learn from their mistakes. I understand that growth often comes with challenges and setbacks, so I foster a culture of resilience and perseverance within the team.

I've seen firsthand the positive impact of these leadership practices on my team. By prioritizing their growth and development, I've witnessed increased motivation, higher job satisfaction, and improved performance across the board. Investing in the training and development of my support staff benefits them individually, strengthens our team, and contributes to the overall success of my business.

Conclusion: Investing in Support Staff Development

As I wrap up this chapter on investing in support staff development, I can't help but reflect on the journey we've taken together. We've explored various strategies and techniques to enhance the skills and capabilities of our support teams, recognizing their pivotal role in delivering exceptional customer experiences.

Throughout our discussion, we've underscored the importance of continuous learning and development in the support industry. From empathy training to technical skill enhancement, we've seen how investing in our team's growth can translate into improved customer satisfaction and loyalty.

By prioritizing training and development initiatives, organizations can empower their support staff to handle a diverse range of customer interactions with confidence and competence. We've discussed the significance of creating a supportive environment where team members feel encouraged to learn, grow, and innovate.

As I bring this chapter to a close, I want to reinforce the value of investing in the training and development of support staff. Not only does it benefit individual team members, but it also strengthens the organization as a whole, driving higher levels of customer satisfaction and long-term success.

I urge organizations to take action and prioritize ongoing learning and growth opportunities for their support teams. Whether it's through formal training programs, mentorship initiatives, or self-directed learning resources, investing in support staff development is an investment in the future of your business. Together, let's continue to elevate customer support standards and drive positive outcomes for our organizations and the customers we serve.

3

MULTICHANNEL SUPPORT STRATEGIES

In today's interconnected world, providing support to customers isn't just about answering phone calls or responding to emails. It's about being available where your customers are, whether on social media, via live chat, or through traditional channels like phone and email. This is where multichannel support comes into play.

Multichannel support refers to the practice of offering assistance and resolving customer issues across various communication channels. It recognizes that customers have different preferences when it comes to seeking support, and businesses need to be present on multiple platforms to meet their diverse needs.

The significance of multichannel support cannot be overstated. In a competitive marketplace where customer experience is a key differentiator, businesses must adapt to the evolving preferences of their clientele. By providing support across multiple channels, companies demonstrate their commitment to accessibility and responsiveness, ultimately enhancing customer satisfaction and loyalty.

This chapter will explore the strategies and best practices for optimizing multichannel support. From understanding the different support channels to integrating support systems and leveraging data analytics, we will delve into the intricacies of multichannel support and provide actionable insights for businesses looking to enhance their customer service operations. So, let's embark on this journey to discover how to effectively navigate the multichannel landscape and deliver exceptional support experiences to our valued customers.

Understanding Multichannel Support Channels

Understanding the landscape of multichannel support means recognizing the different avenues through which customers seek assistance. These channels encompass a spectrum of mediums, each with its unique characteristics and advantages.

Firstly, there's the traditional method of support: the phone. Many customers still prefer the immediacy and personal touch of speaking directly with a representative over the phone. Whether it's for urgent issues or detailed inquiries, the phone remains a cornerstone of customer support.

Then, we have email, a widely used communication tool for both customers and businesses. Email offers a convenient way for customers to articulate their concerns in writing, providing a record of the conversation for future reference. It's a channel favored for more complex issues that may require detailed explanations or documentation.

In recent years, social media has emerged as a prominent support channel. Platforms like Twitter and Facebook have become arenas where customers voice their opinions and seek assistance from brands publicly. Social media offers the advantage of real-time interaction and the ability to showcase transparency and responsiveness to a wider audience.

Live chat is another popular support option, offering instantaneous assistance to customers browsing a website. It provides a seamless way for customers to get quick answers to their questions without picking up the phone or sending an email. Live chat is particularly effective for addressing immediate concerns and guiding users through the purchasing process.

Beyond these primary channels, there are also specialized mediums like SMS messaging, chatbots, and self-service portals, each catering to specific customer preferences and needs.

Understanding the diverse array of support channels is essential for businesses looking to deliver comprehensive and accessible customer service. By embracing a multichannel approach, organizations can meet customers where they are and provide tailored support experiences that drive satisfaction and loyalty.

When it comes to multichannel support, each avenue has its own set of advantages and challenges. Let's break them down.

Firstly, the phone is great for that personal touch. You get to speak directly with someone, which can be reassuring for customers. However, it also means longer wait times during busy periods; sometimes, issues can get lost in translation.

Email is handy because it provides a written record of the conversation, making it easy to refer back to. But it's not as immediate as a phone call, and sometimes messages can get buried in overflowing inboxes.

Social media is fantastic for reaching a wide audience quickly and publicly addressing concerns. It's a bit like putting out fires in a crowded room – everyone sees it. However, managing social media can be time-consuming, and negative feedback can spread like wildfire if not handled promptly.

Live chat is like having someone right there with you while you browse a website. It's quick and convenient, but it requires staff to be available around the clock to provide real-time assistance.

Now, onto the importance of consistency. No matter which channel customers choose, they expect the same level of service. Whether they're calling in or sending a tweet, they want their issue resolved promptly and professionally.

Consistency builds trust. If a customer knows they can rely on your brand to deliver consistent support regardless of the channel, they're more likely to stick around.

However, consistency doesn't mean one-size-fits-all. Each channel has its nuances, and it's essential to tailor your approach accordingly. For example, the tone you use on social media might be more casual than in a formal email response.

Providing consistent and high-quality support across all channels is key to delivering an exceptional customer experience. It's about meeting customers where they are and exceeding their expectations every step of the way.

Tailoring the Customer Experience for Each Channel

Understanding how the customer experience varies across different support channels is crucial for providing exceptional service. Each channel offers a unique interaction with its own set of expectations and challenges.

When customers call our support line, they expect a personal touch. They want to speak with a real person who can empathize with their concerns and provide immediate assistance. It's our opportunity to build rapport and reassure them that we're here to help.

On the other hand, email support offers a more formal and structured communication style. Customers appreciate the convenience of being able to reach out at any time and receive a written response. However, ensuring our emails are clear, concise, and address the customer's issue comprehensively is essential.

Social media support adds another layer to the customer experience. It's fast-paced and public, so our responses must be prompt and professional. Customers expect us to be active and engaged on social platforms, addressing their concerns quickly and transparently.

Live chat support is all about convenience and instant gratification. Customers love the convenience of being able to chat with a support representative in real time while browsing our website. It's an opportunity for us to offer immediate assistance and guide them through any issues they may encounter.

Tailoring the customer experience for each channel means understanding the unique dynamics at play and adapting our approach accordingly. It's about meeting customers where they are and providing the level of service they expect, whether they're calling, emailing, reaching out on social media, or chatting live. By doing so, we can ensure a consistent and positive experience across all support channels, ultimately enhancing customer satisfaction and loyalty.

Adapting our support interactions to fit the characteristics of each channel is essential for delivering a seamless customer experience. Different channels have their own unique quirks and requirements, so it's crucial to tailor our approach accordingly.

I emphasize the importance of active listening and clear communication for phone support. Since customers can't see facial expressions or body language over the phone, I focus on using a friendly and reassuring tone to convey empathy and understanding. It's about being attentive to their needs and providing clear and concise solutions to their problems.

When it comes to email support, I prioritize clarity and thoroughness. Since emails are written communication, I make sure to address all aspects of the customer's inquiry in a structured and organized manner. I avoid jargon and technical language, opting instead for plain language that's easy for the customer to understand.

Social media support requires a different approach altogether. It's fast-paced and public, so I respond quickly and professionally to customer inquiries and comments. I also take advantage of multimedia elements like emojis and gifs to add a personal touch to my responses. It's about engaging with customers in a way that feels authentic and human.

Live chat support is all about being responsive and helpful in real time. I make sure to respond promptly to incoming chat requests and provide timely assistance throughout the conversation. I also utilize canned responses and chatbots to streamline the support process and ensure consistency across interactions.

While adapting to each channel's unique characteristics, it's important to maintain brand consistency. This means adhering to our brand voice and values while also being mindful of the nuances of each channel. By striking the right balance between consistency and channel-specific adaptation, we can ensure that our customers receive the same high-quality support experience, no matter how they choose to reach out to us.

Integration of Multichannel Support Systems

Integrating multichannel support systems has been a game-changer for our business. It's all about bringing together different communication channels into one seamless platform, making it easier for us to manage customer inquiries and provide timely responses.

One of the biggest benefits of integration is efficiency. Having all support channels centralized in one system can streamline our workflow and reduce the risk of overlooking or duplicating customer inquiries. This means fewer missed opportunities and faster resolution times, ultimately leading to happier customers.

Another advantage is consistency. With an integrated system, we can ensure that our responses are consistent across all channels. Whether a customer reaches out via email, social media, or live chat, they can expect the same level of professionalism and quality of service. This consistency helps to strengthen our brand reputation and build trust with our customers.

Integration also allows us to gather valuable insights into customer behavior and preferences. By tracking interactions across different channels, we can identify trends and patterns that help us better understand our customers' needs and preferences. This, in turn, allows us to tailor our support strategies to better meet their expectations.

Overall, integrating multichannel support systems has been a game-changer for our business. It has helped us improve efficiency, consistency, and customer satisfaction, ultimately driving growth and success.

When it comes to managing multichannel support operations, technology is our best friend. It's what helps us keep everything running smoothly and ensures that we can provide top-notch service to our customers across all channels.

There are a variety of technology solutions out there designed specifically for streamlining multichannel support operations. One example is customer relationship management (CRM) software, which allows us to centralize customer data and interactions, making it easier to track and manage inquiries from different channels in one place. With CRM, we can access customer information quickly and efficiently, which helps us provide personalized and timely support.

Another valuable technology solution is helpdesk software. This type of software is designed to handle customer inquiries from various channels, such as email, live chat, and social media, all within one platform. Helpdesk software often includes features like ticket management, automation, and reporting, which help us improve our response times and overall efficiency.

We also utilize tools like Slack or Microsoft Teams to facilitate internal communication and collaboration among support team members. These tools allow us to quickly share information, ask questions, and coordinate responses to customer inquiries, ensuring everyone is on the same page and working together effectively.

Overall, technology plays a crucial role in streamlining our multichannel support operations. By leveraging the right tools and solutions, we can provide efficient, consistent, and high-quality support to our customers across all channels, ultimately driving satisfaction and loyalty.

Selecting and implementing integrated support platforms can initially seem daunting, but with the right approach, it becomes a manageable task that can greatly benefit our operations.

When choosing a platform, it's important to consider our specific needs and requirements. We need to assess factors such as the volume of support inquiries we receive, the channels our customers prefer to use, and the level of customization and scalability we require. By understanding our unique needs, we can narrow down our options and focus on platforms that align closely with what we're looking for.

It's also essential to thoroughly research and evaluate the features and capabilities of each platform under consideration. We need to look beyond the basic functionalities and assess factors like ease of use, integration with existing systems, reporting and analytics capabilities, and customer support offerings. This ensures we choose a platform that meets our current needs and has the flexibility to grow and adapt with our business over time.

Once we've selected a platform, the implementation process begins. It's important to approach implementation with careful planning and attention to detail. This involves setting clear objectives and timelines, allocating resources effectively, and communicating with stakeholders throughout the process. We may also need to provide training and support to our team members to ensure they are comfortable and proficient with the new platform.

Throughout the implementation process, it's important to stay flexible and adaptable. There may be unforeseen challenges or roadblocks along the way, but by remaining open-minded and responsive, we can address these issues effectively and keep the implementation on track.

By following these tips and approaching the selection and implementation of integrated support platforms thoughtfully and strategically, we can ensure that we choose the right solution for our business and maximize the benefits of multichannel support for our customers.

Managing Customer Expectations Across Channels

Managing customer expectations across various channels is paramount in ensuring a positive experience for our clients. When customers reach out for support, they expect timely and efficient responses, regardless of their communication channel. As a business owner, I recognize the importance of setting clear expectations regarding each channel's response times and service levels.

Customers should know what to expect when they contact us through different channels such as phone, email, social media, or live chat. By clearly defining response times and service levels for each channel, we can manage customer expectations effectively and provide a consistent level of service across all touchpoints.

For example, if we promise a response within 24 hours for email inquiries, we must ensure that we deliver on that promise consistently. Similarly, if we offer live chat support during certain hours, we must clearly communicate those hours to customers so they know when they can expect a response.

Setting clear expectations helps manage customer perceptions and enables us to prioritize and allocate resources effectively. By understanding the expected response times for each channel, we can ensure that we have the necessary staff and resources in place to meet customer needs promptly.

Moreover, clear communication of service levels and response times fosters transparency and trust with our customers. When customers know what to expect, they are more likely to feel satisfied with the level of service they receive, even if their issue cannot be resolved immediately.

In summary, setting clear expectations for response times and service levels across all support channels is essential for managing customer perceptions, allocating resources effectively, and building trust with our clients. As a business owner, I am committed to meeting and exceeding customer expectations across all communication channels.

Communicating channel-specific support policies to our customers is crucial for ensuring a smooth and transparent experience. As a business owner, I understand the importance of effectively communicating our policies and procedures across all support channels.

One strategy we employ is clearly outlining our website's support policies, including information on response times, available channels, and escalation procedures. By providing this information upfront, customers can easily access and understand our support processes before reaching out for assistance.

In addition to our website, we also use automated email responses and pre-chat messages to communicate channel-specific policies to customers. When a customer submits a support request via email or initiates a live chat session, they receive an automated message outlining our response times and directing them to additional resources if needed. This proactive approach helps set expectations right from the start and reduces confusion for our customers.

When it comes to handling customer inquiries and escalations across multiple channels, we prioritize consistency and efficiency. Our support team is trained to provide the same level of service and attention to detail regardless of the channel through which the inquiry is received.

For example, if a customer contacts us via social media with an urgent issue, we ensure that their inquiry is promptly addressed and escalated to the appropriate department if necessary. Similarly, if a customer reaches out via phone or email, our team follows the same protocol to ensure a timely and satisfactory resolution.

We can effectively manage customer inquiries and escalations across all channels by establishing clear communication channels and consistent support processes. Our goal is to provide our customers with a seamless and responsive experience, regardless of how they choose to reach out for assistance.

Leveraging Data Analytics for Multichannel Support

In my business, we've embraced the power of data analytics to gain valuable insights into how we're performing across our various support channels. It's like having a behind-the-scenes view of our customer interactions, allowing us to make informed decisions and improvements.

When we talk about data analytics, we're essentially referring to the process of collecting, analyzing, and interpreting data to understand patterns, trends, and customer behavior. It's not just about crunching numbers; it's about extracting meaningful insights that can drive our business forward.

We can track key performance indicators (KPIs) such as response times, resolution rates, and customer satisfaction scores across different channels by leveraging data analytics for multichannel support. This information gives us a comprehensive picture of how we're performing and where we might need to adjust.

For example, let's say we notice a spike in customer inquiries on social media during certain times of the day. With data analytics, we can drill down further to understand the nature of these inquiries and whether we need to allocate more resources to handle them efficiently.

Additionally, data analytics can help us identify trends and patterns in customer behavior, allowing us to anticipate their needs and preferences. For instance, if we notice a growing demand for live chat support among our customers, we can prioritize resources to ensure a seamless experience across this channel.

Overall, leveraging data analytics for multichannel support enables us to make data-driven decisions that ultimately lead to better customer experiences. It's like having a compass that guides us in the right direction, helping us navigate the ever-changing landscape of customer support with confidence and precision.

In our business, we've come to understand that to truly gauge the effectiveness of our multichannel support efforts, we need to focus on the right metrics and key performance indicators (KPIs). It's not just about how many calls we handle or how quickly we respond to emails; it's about measuring what really matters in terms of customer satisfaction and business success.

When we talk about key metrics and KPIs for evaluating multichannel support effectiveness, we're looking at indicators that give us insights into how well we're meeting our customer's needs and expectations across different channels.

One important metric is response time, which measures how quickly we can acknowledge and respond to customer inquiries or issues. Whether it's through email, phone, live chat, or social media, our goal is to provide timely responses that show our customers we're here to help.

Another crucial metric is the resolution rate, which assesses our ability to effectively resolve customer issues on the first contact. This metric reflects the efficiency of our support team and indicates how well we understand and address customer needs.

Customer satisfaction scores are also essential KPIs for evaluating multichannel support effectiveness. By collecting customer feedback after their support interactions, we can gauge their level of satisfaction with the service received and identify areas for improvement.

Furthermore, we look at channel-specific metrics to understand how each support channel is performing individually. For example, we might track the number of interactions on social media versus email or compare the average resolution times across different channels.

Ultimately, by focusing on these key metrics and KPIs, we can gain a comprehensive understanding of our multichannel support effectiveness and make data-driven decisions to continuously improve the customer experience. It's about keeping our finger on the pulse of customer satisfaction and using that insight to drive positive change in our support operations.

In our business, harnessing the power of data analytics has become essential for staying ahead of the curve. It's not just about collecting data; it's about using that data to uncover valuable insights that can drive meaningful improvements in our multichannel support operations.

One technique we use is trend analysis, where we examine historical data to identify patterns and trends in customer interactions. By analyzing trends such as spikes in customer inquiries during certain times of the day or week, we can better anticipate and prepare for high-demand periods, ensuring we have adequate resources in place to handle incoming requests promptly.

Another valuable technique is sentiment analysis, which involves analyzing customer feedback to understand the tone and sentiment behind their interactions. By using natural language processing algorithms, we can categorize customer feedback as positive, negative, or neutral, allowing us to pinpoint areas where we're excelling and areas where we need to improve.

Furthermore, predictive analytics plays a crucial role in helping us forecast future support trends and customer behavior. By analyzing historical data and identifying patterns, we can make informed predictions about future customer needs and preferences, allowing us to proactively address potential issues before they escalate.

Additionally, data visualization techniques, such as dashboards and heat maps, help us present complex data in a visually appealing and easy-to-understand format. These visualizations allow us to quickly identify areas for improvement and track our progress toward key performance indicators.

Overall, leveraging data analytics empowers us to make data-driven decisions that drive continuous improvement in our multichannel support operations. By harnessing the insights gleaned from data analysis, we can enhance the customer experience, optimize resource allocation, and stay ahead of the competition in today's fast-paced business landscape.

Training and Empowering Support Teams for Multichannel Support

Ensuring that our support teams are well-equipped to handle multichannel interactions is paramount to our success. As the landscape of customer service continues to evolve, it's crucial that our teams are not only proficient in traditional support channels like phone and email but also adept at navigating newer channels such as social media and live chat.

Comprehensive training is the cornerstone of preparing our support teams for the challenges of multichannel support. Through structured training programs, we provide our team members with the knowledge and skills they need to effectively engage with customers across various channels. This includes training on each channel's unique features and functionalities, as well as best practices for delivering exceptional service regardless of the platform.

One of the key aspects of our training approach is hands-on practice. We believe that the best way for our team members to learn is by doing, so we provide ample opportunities for them to practice their skills in a simulated environment. Through role-playing exercises and scenario-based simulations, our team members can confidently hone their communication skills and learn how to navigate real-world support scenarios.

Moreover, empowering our support teams is essential for success in multichannel support. Empowerment means giving our team members the autonomy and authority to make decisions and solve problems independently. By empowering our teams, we foster a sense of ownership and accountability, ultimately leading to higher customer satisfaction and loyalty.

In addition to training and empowerment, ongoing support and feedback are crucial for the continued development of our support teams. We regularly provide coaching and mentoring to help our team members continuously improve their skills and address any challenges they may encounter.

Overall, by investing in comprehensive training and empowerment for our support teams, we position ourselves to deliver exceptional multichannel support experiences that drive customer satisfaction and loyalty.

Our priority is empowering our support agents to navigate and resolve issues across various channels. We understand that each channel comes with its unique set of challenges, and it's essential for our agents to feel confident and capable of addressing customer inquiries, regardless of the platform.

To achieve this, we implement strategies aimed at empowering our support agents to excel in multichannel interactions. One key strategy is providing comprehensive training that equips our agents with the skills and knowledge they need to effectively handle customer issues across different channels. This includes training on channel-specific tools and technologies and strategies for managing customer interactions in real time.

In addition to training, we also focus on fostering a culture of empowerment within our support teams. We encourage our agents to take ownership of customer issues and empower them to make decisions autonomously when resolving customer inquiries. By giving our agents the authority to take action, we enable them to provide faster and more efficient support, ultimately leading to higher levels of customer satisfaction.

Furthermore, we recognize the importance of collaboration and knowledge sharing among our support teams in a multichannel environment. To facilitate this, we implement various initiatives aimed at promoting teamwork and information exchange. This includes regular team meetings, where agents can discuss challenges and share best practices, as well as collaborative tools and platforms for sharing information and resources.

By empowering our support agents and fostering collaboration among teams, we create an environment where our agents feel confident and supported in providing exceptional support across all channels. This not only enhances the customer experience but also contributes to the overall success of our business.

CASE STUDIES AND EXAMPLES

In our exploration of multichannel support strategies, we find immense value in real-life examples that showcase how organizations effectively navigate the complexities of managing support across multiple channels. These case studies provide valuable insights into the practical application of multichannel support strategies and offer inspiration for our own endeavors.

One noteworthy example is a leading e-commerce company that seamlessly integrates various support channels, including phone, email, live chat, and social media. By offering multiple avenues for customer interaction, they ensure accessibility and convenience for their diverse customer base. Their multichannel approach has significantly improved customer satisfaction and retention rates, demonstrating the importance of catering to customer preferences.

However, along with success stories come challenges, and we acknowledge the importance of learning from both triumphs and setbacks. Another case study highlights a software company that initially struggled to manage multichannel support operations effectively due to siloed systems and disjointed processes. However, by investing in integrated support platforms and providing comprehensive training for their support teams, they overcame these challenges and delivered exceptional support experiences across all channels.

Furthermore, insights from industry leaders offer valuable guidance on best practices for optimizing multichannel support. By learning from the experiences and expertise of those who have navigated similar challenges, we gain valuable insights that can inform our strategies and approaches. These insights help us stay informed of emerging trends and innovations in multichannel support, ensuring that we remain agile and responsive to evolving customer needs.

Overall, case studies and examples serve as powerful tools for understanding the complexities of multichannel support and uncovering strategies for success. By studying real-life examples, we gain practical insights that inform our own approach to managing multichannel support operations and drive continuous improvement in our customer service efforts.

Conclusion: Maximizing Multichannel Support Effectiveness

As we wrap up our exploration of multichannel support strategies, I'm reminded of the key takeaways that underscore the significance of embracing this approach in our customer service efforts.

Throughout this chapter, we've delved into various aspects of multichannel support, from understanding its definition and importance to tailoring the customer experience across different channels. We've discussed the benefits of integrating support systems and leveraging data analytics to gain insights into performance. Additionally, we've explored the critical role of training and empowering support teams to navigate multichannel interactions effectively.

Reflecting on these insights, it becomes evident that in today's customer-centric landscape, offering support across multiple channels is not just advantageous but necessary. Customers expect accessibility and convenience, and by meeting them where they are, we can foster stronger relationships and drive loyalty.

As we move forward, it's crucial for organizations to prioritize the development and implementation of multichannel support strategies. By doing so, we can enhance customer satisfaction and loyalty, ultimately driving business success.

In conclusion, let's commit to maximizing the effectiveness of our multichannel support efforts. By embracing this approach and continuously refining our strategies, we can create meaningful experiences that resonate with our customers and set us apart in the competitive marketplace.

4
MEASURING CUSTOMER SUPPORT SUCCESS

When we talk about measuring customer support success, we're essentially looking at how well we're meeting our customers' needs and expectations. It's about assessing our performance in providing assistance, resolving issues, and ensuring customer satisfaction.

Tracking and evaluating customer support performance is crucial for any business. It helps us understand where we're excelling and where we need to improve. By measuring our effectiveness in supporting customers, we can identify areas for enhancement, streamline processes, and ultimately deliver better service.

In this chapter, we'll dive into various strategies for measuring and enhancing customer support effectiveness. We'll explore different metrics and methods for evaluating performance, from response times to customer satisfaction scores. By the end of this chapter, you'll have a toolkit of approaches to gauge and elevate your customer support game.

Key Metrics for Evaluating Customer Support Performance

When it comes to evaluating our customer support performance, there are a few key metrics that we need to pay close attention to. These metrics give us valuable insights into how well we're serving our customers and where we might need to make improvements.

First off, there's response time. This is the time it takes for us to respond to a customer inquiry or issue. It's important because customers want timely assistance, and a quick response can make a big difference in their experience. Then, there's resolution time, which is how long it takes us to fully resolve a customer's problem. Again, speed matters here, but we also want to ensure that we're providing thorough and effective solutions.

Lastly, we have customer satisfaction scores. These scores reflect how happy our customers are with the support they receive. It's not just about solving problems; it's about doing so in a way that leaves customers feeling valued and satisfied. High satisfaction scores indicate that we're meeting or exceeding expectations, while low scores might signal areas where we need to improve our service.

Each of these metrics tells us something different about our support quality. Response time and resolution time give us insights into efficiency and effectiveness, while customer satisfaction scores offer a glimpse into overall satisfaction and loyalty. By tracking and analyzing these metrics, we can better understand our performance and take steps to continuously improve our customer support efforts.

In our quest to provide top-notch customer support, my team and I are always looking for ways to raise the bar. One effective strategy we've adopted is benchmarking and goal-setting. Let me break it down for you.

Benchmarking involves comparing our performance metrics against industry standards or against our past performance. It's like checking the score of our game against others in the league. By benchmarking, we can see how we stack up and identify areas where we excel and where we could use some improvement.

Once we have a clear picture of where we stand, it's time to set some goals. These goals should be specific, measurable, achievable, relevant, and time-bound (SMART). For example, we might set a goal to reduce our average response time by 20% within the next quarter. Having clear goals gives us something to strive for and helps keep us focused on continuous improvement.

But it's not just about setting goals; it's also about tracking our progress toward them. We regularly monitor our performance metrics and adjust our strategies as needed to stay on track. When we hit our goals, we celebrate our successes and set new goals to keep pushing ourselves forward.

By incorporating benchmarking and goal setting into our customer support strategy, we're able to drive performance improvements and deliver even better service to our customers. It's all about setting the bar high and constantly striving to raise it.

Implementing Customer Feedback Mechanisms

In our pursuit of excellence in customer support, we've come to realize the immense value of listening to our customers. That's why we've made it a priority to implement robust feedback mechanisms. We set up various channels for customers to share their thoughts and experiences with us. We use surveys, reviews, and feedback forms, making it easy for them to reach out and let us know how we're doing. This two-way communication is crucial because it allows us to understand our customers' needs and concerns directly from the source.

However, it's not just about collecting feedback; it's about what we do with it. We take the time to analyze the feedback we receive, looking for patterns and trends that can help us improve our support performance. Whether identifying common pain points or recognizing areas where we excel, this feedback is like a compass guiding us in the right direction.

By continuously gathering and analyzing customer feedback, we're able to stay agile and responsive to our customers' ever-changing needs. It's a key part of our commitment to providing exceptional support and ensuring that every interaction leaves our customers feeling heard and valued.

In our business, we've learned that collecting customer feedback is just the first step. The real magic happens when we turn that feedback into actionable insights that drive meaningful change. Here's how we do it.

One strategy we've found effective is to involve our support team in the feedback process. They're on the front lines, interacting with customers daily, so they have valuable firsthand insights to share. We hold regular meetings where team members can discuss the feedback they've received and brainstorm ways to address any recurring issues or concerns.

Another key strategy is to prioritize feedback that highlights areas for improvement. While positive feedback is always nice to receive, constructive criticism helps us grow. By focusing on the feedback that points out areas where we can do better, we can make targeted improvements that impact the customer experience.

We also make sure to follow up with customers after implementing changes based on their feedback. This shows them that we're listening and that their input matters to us. It's a great way to foster trust and loyalty while ensuring our changes have the desired effect.

Incorporating customer feedback into our support processes isn't just about checking a box; it's about constantly striving to improve. By listening to our customers, involving our team, and prioritizing actionable insights, we can create a support experience that truly sets us apart.

Utilizing Data Analytics for Performance Insights

In our business, we've come to rely heavily on data analytics to gain insights into our support performance. Let me tell you why.

First off, data analytics tools allow us to take all the raw data we collect—like customer interactions, response times, and resolution rates—and turn it into actionable insights. These insights help us understand where we excel and have room for improvement.

For example, let's say we notice a spike in customer inquiries about a particular product feature. By digging into the data, we might discover that there's a common issue causing confusion among users. Armed with this knowledge, we can proactively address the issue, whether it's through additional training for our support team or updates to our product documentation.

However, data analytics isn't just about identifying problems—it's also about uncovering opportunities. By analyzing trends over time, we can spot areas where we consistently exceed expectations and double down on those strengths. This might mean reallocating resources to focus more on the channels or support methods that are proving most effective.

One of the things I love most about data analytics is its ability to provide real-time insights. With the right tools in place, we can monitor our support performance in real time, allowing us to quickly identify and address any issues that arise. It's like having a finger on the pulse of our customer support operation at all times.

Overall, data analytics has become an indispensable tool for managing our support operations. By harnessing the power of data, we're able to make smarter decisions, deliver better service to our customers, and ultimately drive greater success for our business.

In our journey to improve our customer support, we've learned that it's not just about collecting data—it's about using that data to make real improvements. Let me share how we've been able to turn our support data into actionable insights.

When we talk about extracting actionable insights, we're talking about digging deep into the data to uncover patterns and trends that can guide our decision-making. For example, let's say we notice a recurring issue that's causing a spike in customer inquiries. By analyzing the data, we can identify the root cause of the problem and take steps to address it, whether that's through additional training for our support team or updates to our product.

But it's not just about fixing problems—it's also about finding opportunities for improvement. Maybe we notice that certain support channels are more effective than others at resolving customer issues. Armed with this knowledge, we can allocate our resources more effectively, ensuring that we're investing in the channels that deliver the best results.

Let me share a couple of case studies to bring this concept to life. In one instance, we noticed a significant increase in customer satisfaction scores after implementing a new support workflow based on insights from our data analysis. By streamlining our processes and focusing on the areas that mattered most to our customers, we were able to make a real impact on their experience.

In another case, we used data-driven decision-making to identify a bottleneck in our support operations. By reorganizing our team and implementing new tools, we significantly reduced response times and improved overall customer satisfaction.

These case studies highlight the power of data-driven decision-making in driving improvements in customer support. By leveraging our support data to its fullest potential, we've made smarter decisions, delivered better service to our customers, and ultimately drove greater success for our business.

Assessing Team Productivity and Efficiency

Assessing the productivity and efficiency of our support team is crucial to ensuring we're delivering the best service possible to our customers. Let me explain how we measure and evaluate our team's performance.

One key metric we focus on is ticket volume. This metric tells us how many customer inquiries our team is handling within a given period. By tracking ticket volume over time, we can identify trends and patterns in customer demand, allowing us to allocate resources more effectively and anticipate busy periods.

Another important metric is agent workload. This measures the number of tickets each support agent is handling at any given time. High agent workload can indicate that our team is stretched too thin, leading to longer response times and lower-quality support. By monitoring agent workload, we can ensure that our team is properly staffed to handle incoming inquiries without becoming overwhelmed.

However, it's not just about quantity; we also pay attention to the quality of our support interactions. Metrics like first response and resolution times help us gauge how quickly and effectively we address customer issues. We can hold ourselves accountable and strive for continuous improvement by setting goals and benchmarks for these metrics.

By regularly assessing team productivity and efficiency through these metrics, we can identify areas for improvement and make data-driven decisions to optimize our support operations. This allows us to provide faster, more effective customer support, ultimately leading to higher satisfaction and loyalty.

When it comes to optimizing our team's efficiency and managing workload, we've found a few strategies that really make a difference. Let me share some insights into how we keep things running smoothly.

First off, we focus on streamlining our processes wherever possible. This means identifying repetitive tasks or bottlenecks in our workflow and finding ways to automate or simplify them. By reducing manual work, we can free up time for our team to focus on more high-value tasks, like resolving complex customer issues or providing personalized support.

Another key strategy is effective workload management. We make sure to distribute incoming tickets evenly among our team members, taking into account factors like expertise and availability. This helps prevent any one agent from feeling overwhelmed and ensures that every customer inquiry receives prompt attention.

It's not just about getting through tickets as quickly as possible. We also prioritize quality in our support interactions. That means taking the time to truly understand our customers' needs and providing thoughtful, helpful responses. Sometimes, that might mean spending a little extra time on a ticket to ensure we're delivering the best possible solution.

Balancing productivity with quality is essential for maintaining customer satisfaction and loyalty. While we want to be efficient and responsive, we also recognize that rushing through tickets can lead to mistakes or oversights. That's why we emphasize the importance of finding the right balance between speed and accuracy in our support efforts.

By implementing these strategies and keeping a close eye on our team's efficiency and workload, we're able to provide top-notch support that our customers can rely on. It's all about finding that sweet spot where we're delivering fast, effective assistance while also ensuring we're meeting our customers' expectations for quality and care.

Monitoring and Improving Customer Satisfaction

When it comes to keeping our customers happy, measuring satisfaction is key. We want to know how we're doing so we can make any necessary improvements and keep providing the best experience possible.

One way we do this is through surveys. After a support interaction, we'll often send out a quick questionnaire to gather feedback from the customer. These surveys ask questions about their experience, like how satisfied they were with the assistance they received and if there's anything we could have done better. By collecting this feedback directly from our customers, we can clearly understand what we're doing well and where we might need to focus on improving.

Another metric we use is the Net Promoter Score, or NPS. This measures how likely a customer is to recommend our product or service to others. We'll often include an NPS question in our surveys, asking customers to rate on a scale of 0 to 10 how likely they are to recommend us to a friend or colleague. This gives us valuable insight into how satisfied our customers are and how likely they are to become advocates for our brand.

However, it's not just about collecting data; it's about using that data to drive improvements. We take action when we see areas where our customers aren't as satisfied as we'd like them to be. That might mean making changes to our processes, providing additional training to our support team, or even making updates to our product or service based on customer feedback.

Ultimately, our goal is to continually monitor and improve customer satisfaction. By staying proactive and responsive to our customer's needs, we can ensure that they're happy and that they'll keep coming back to us for all their support needs.

As a business owner, I've learned that promptly addressing customer feedback is essential for keeping our customers happy and loyal. When a customer takes the time to provide feedback or raises an issue, it's a valuable opportunity for us to show that we care about their experience and are committed to making things right.

When we receive feedback or hear about an issue from a customer, we prioritize responding quickly and addressing their concerns. Whether it's a complaint about a product or service, a suggestion for improvement, or simply a question that needs answering, we want our customers to know that we're listening and that we're here to help.

By promptly addressing customer feedback, we resolve individual issues and demonstrate our commitment to customer satisfaction. This can go a long way in building trust and loyalty with our customers, as they see that we're responsive and dedicated to providing a positive experience.

In addition to addressing feedback reactively, we also take proactive steps to enhance customer satisfaction and loyalty. One strategy we use is to anticipate our customer's needs and provide support before they even have to ask for it. This might mean reaching out to customers with helpful tips or resources, proactively addressing common issues before they become problems, or offering personalized recommendations based on their past interactions with us.

Another tip for enhancing customer satisfaction is to focus on building customer relationships. We aim to treat every interaction as an opportunity to strengthen our relationship with the customer, whether it's through friendly and helpful support interactions, personalized communication, or going the extra mile to exceed their expectations.

Ultimately, by addressing customer feedback promptly and proactively focusing on enhancing satisfaction, we can build stronger relationships with our customers and foster greater loyalty to our brand. In today's competitive business landscape, loyal customers are the key to long-term success.

Analyzing Cost-Effectiveness and ROI

In my experience running a business, understanding the cost-effectiveness of our customer support operations is crucial for maintaining profitability while still delivering excellent service to our customers. When we talk about cost-effectiveness, we're looking at how efficiently we're using our resources to provide support and whether the benefits outweigh the costs.

One metric we use to assess cost-effectiveness is the cost per interaction. This metric helps us understand how much we're spending on average to handle each customer inquiry or issue. By tracking this metric over time, we can identify trends and areas where we may be able to improve efficiency and reduce costs.

Another important metric is the return on investment (ROI) of our customer support efforts. This involves comparing the benefits of providing support—such as increased customer satisfaction, retention, and loyalty—to the costs involved in delivering that support. For example, suppose we invest in implementing a new support tool or hiring additional support staff. In that case, we want to ensure that the benefits we receive from these investments justify the costs.

In addition to these metrics, we also look at factors like customer lifetime value (CLV) and customer acquisition cost

(CAC) to get a more holistic view of the financial impact of our customer support operations. By understanding how much it costs to acquire and retain customers and how much revenue they generate over their lifetime with us, we can make more informed decisions about where to allocate our resources for maximum impact.

Analyzing cost-effectiveness and ROI isn't just about cutting costs—it's about finding the right balance between providing excellent support to our customers and managing our resources efficiently. By tracking these metrics and continually optimizing our processes, we can ensure that we're delivering the best possible service to our customers while also running a financially sustainable business.

In managing my business, one of the ongoing challenges is optimizing our resource allocation to ensure we're effectively managing support costs while still delivering top-notch service to our customers. It's a delicate balance between keeping expenses in check and providing the level of support our customers expect.

We've developed several strategies for optimizing resource allocation to tackle this challenge. One approach we take is to carefully analyze our support workload and identify areas where we can streamline processes or automate tasks to increase efficiency. By leveraging technology and tools, we can reduce the time and effort required to handle support inquiries, allowing us to serve more customers with the same resources.

Another strategy we employ is cross-training our support team members to handle a wider range of issues. This helps us avoid overstaffing in specific areas and ensures that we can adapt to fluctuations in demand without sacrificing service quality. Additionally, we regularly review our support workflows and procedures to identify any inefficiencies or bottlenecks that may be driving up costs.

When it comes to evaluating the return on investment (ROI) for our customer support initiatives, we take a comprehensive approach. We look at the direct costs associated with providing support, such as salaries and technology expenses, and the indirect benefits, such as increased customer satisfaction and loyalty.

Calculating ROI for customer support initiatives involves comparing the costs incurred with the benefits gained. For example, if we invest in implementing a new support tool, we'll track the upfront costs of purchasing and implementing the tool and any ongoing maintenance expenses. Then, we'll measure the tool's impact on key metrics like response time, resolution time, and customer satisfaction scores.

By evaluating the ROI of our customer support initiatives, we can ensure that we're making smart investments that drive real value for our business. This allows us to allocate our resources more effectively, focusing on initiatives that deliver the highest return and ultimately helping us achieve our goals of providing exceptional customer support while managing costs responsibly.

Benchmarking Against Industry Standards and Competitors

As a business owner, I've learned that staying ahead in the market requires more than just keeping up with the competition—it means continually striving to improve and innovate. One way we do this is by benchmarking our support performance against industry standards and our competitors.

Benchmarking is like taking a snapshot of where we stand in comparison to others in our industry. It helps us understand how well we're doing in terms of customer support and where there's room for improvement. By measuring ourselves against industry standards, we can identify areas where we excel and areas where we may be falling short.

Benchmarking isn't just about keeping tabs on our performance; it's also about understanding how we stack up against our competitors. By analyzing what others in our industry are doing well, we can learn from their successes and identify opportunities to differentiate ourselves in the market.

For example, suppose we notice that our response times are slower than the industry average. In that case, we might invest in improving our support processes or consider hiring additional staff to handle incoming inquiries more efficiently. On the other hand, if we find that our customer satisfaction scores are higher than those of our competitors, we can use that as a selling point to attract new customers and retain existing ones.

Ultimately, benchmarking against industry standards and competitors helps us set realistic goals for our support performance and stay focused on continuous improvement. It's a valuable tool in our arsenal for staying ahead of the curve and delivering the best possible experience to our customers.

In my experience as a business owner, keeping an eye on what my competitors are doing is just smart business. After all, understanding their support practices can give me valuable insights into what's working well in the market and where I might have room to improve.

To identify and analyze my competitors' support practices, I start by researching. I take a look at their websites, read customer reviews, and even reach out to their support teams incognito to experience their service firsthand. This helps me understand how they handle customer inquiries, what channels they offer support through, and what kind of response times they provide.

Once I've gathered this information, I compare it to my support practices. I look for areas where my competitors might be outperforming me, whether in terms of response times, customer satisfaction scores, or the range of support channels they offer. This comparison allows me to identify potential gaps in my support strategy and prioritize areas for improvement.

Benchmarking is also about setting goals for myself based on what I've learned. Armed with this benchmarking data, I can set realistic performance goals for my support team and track our progress over time. For example, suppose I see that my competitors are consistently achieving higher customer satisfaction scores than me. In that case, I might set a goal to improve our own scores by a certain percentage within a specific timeframe.

By leveraging benchmarking data to set performance goals, I can drive improvements in my support operations and stay competitive in the market. It's all about learning from the competition and using that knowledge to push myself and my team to be the best we can be.

Conclusion: Driving Continuous Improvement in Customer Support

As I wrap up this chapter, I can't help but reflect on the journey we've taken together to understand how to measure and improve customer support. We've covered a lot of ground, from identifying key metrics to leveraging data analytics and benchmarking against industry standards. Now, let's take a moment to recap the key insights and strategies that we've discussed.

First and foremost, we've learned the importance of tracking and evaluating customer support performance. Without measuring our success, we're essentially flying blind. By keeping a close eye on metrics like response time, customer satisfaction, and cost-effectiveness, we can identify areas for improvement and ensure that we're providing the best possible support to our customers.

We've also seen how valuable customer feedback can be in driving improvements. We can build stronger relationships and improve overall satisfaction by listening to our customers and addressing their concerns promptly. Incorporating feedback into our support processes ensures we're constantly evolving to meet our customers' needs.

Let's not forget the power of data analytics. By harnessing the insights buried within our support data, we can make more informed decisions and drive meaningful improvements in our operations. Whether it's optimizing team productivity or identifying trends in customer behavior, data analytics gives us the tools we need to stay ahead of the curve.

As we close out this chapter, I want to leave you with a call to action. It's not enough to measure our performance; we must act on what we learn and strive for continuous improvement. By prioritizing performance measurement and implementing strategies for ongoing growth, we can ensure that our customer support remains top-notch in an ever-changing business landscape.

5

BUILDING A CUSTOMER-CENTRIC CULTURE

As we embark on this chapter, let's talk about something foundational to every successful business: a customer-centric culture. You might wonder, what exactly does that mean? Well, put simply, it's about making our customers the heart of everything we do.

When I say "customer-centric culture," I mean creating an environment where every decision and action revolves around meeting and exceeding customer needs and expectations. It's more than just a buzzword; it's a fundamental shift in how we approach business.

Why is this so crucial? In today's highly competitive landscape, where options abound and customer loyalty can be fickle, putting our customers first is the key to standing out and thriving. It's about building trust, fostering loyalty, and ultimately driving long-term growth.

Throughout this chapter, we'll dive into various strategies aimed at nurturing this customer-centric mindset within our organization. From empowering employees to integrating customer feedback into our processes, we'll explore practical steps to embed customer-centricity into the very fabric of our company. So, let's roll up our sleeves and get started on this journey toward building a customer-centric culture that sets us apart from the rest.

Understanding the Importance of Customer-Centricity

Let's talk about why being customer-centric is absolutely essential for our business to thrive. It's not just a nice-to-have; it's a must-have in today's competitive marketplace.

Being customer-centric means putting our customers at the forefront of everything we do. It's about truly understanding their needs, preferences, and pain points and tailoring our products, services, and experiences to meet and exceed those expectations.

Why does this matter so much? Well, for starters, it's all about loyalty. When customers feel like they're truly valued and understood, they're more likely to stick around and keep coming back for more. And not only that, but they're also more likely to sing our praises to others, becoming advocates for our brand.

However, it's not just about retaining customers; it's also about attracting new ones. In today's digital age, where word-of-mouth travels at lightning speed through social media and online reviews, a stellar reputation for customer-centricity can be a powerful magnet for new business.

And let's not forget about the bottom line. Studies have consistently shown that companies with a strong focus on customer-centricity tend to outperform their competitors in terms of revenue and profitability. Why? Because happy customers are more willing to spend more, more often.

So, when we talk about the importance of customer-centricity, it's not just about being nice to our customers (although that's certainly part of it). It's about driving real, tangible business results that can propel us forward in the marketplace.

Let's dive into why prioritizing customer needs and experiences can make a difference for our business.

First off, when we prioritize our customers, it's not just about making them happy in the moment. It's about building relationships that last. By consistently delivering exceptional experiences, we're showing our customers that we value them, are here to serve them, and are committed to meeting their needs.

Happy customers are loyal customers. When we go above and beyond to exceed their expectations, they're more likely to stick with us, even when faced with tempting offers from competitors. That loyalty translates into repeat business, which, in turn, drives long-term growth and profitability.

However, it's not just about retaining customers; it's also about attracting new ones. A reputation for outstanding customer service and satisfaction can be a powerful marketing tool. Happy customers are more likely to recommend us to their friends, family, and colleagues, helping us expand our customer base without spending a fortune on advertising.

Plus, when we're truly focused on our customers' needs and experiences, it's easier to spot opportunities for innovation and improvement. We can identify pain points and areas for enhancement and then take action to address them. This continuous cycle of listening, learning, and adapting is key to staying ahead of the curve in today's fast-paced business world.

Therefore, when we talk about the benefits of building a customer-centric culture, it's not just about being nice to our customers (although that's certainly important). It's about driving sustainable growth, fostering loyalty, and staying competitive in an ever-evolving marketplace.

Leadership's Role in Creating a Customer-Centric Culture

As the leader of our organization, I've come to understand just how pivotal my role is in shaping our culture. When it comes to fostering a customer-centric environment, the responsibility falls squarely on my shoulders.

As leaders, we set the tone for the entire company. Our actions and attitudes trickle down and influence every aspect of the organization. So, if we want to create a culture that truly prioritizes our customers, it starts with us.

One of the most important things I've learned is the power of leading by example. I can talk all day long about the importance of customer satisfaction, but if my actions don't align with those words, they'll fall flat. That's why I make it a point to always put our customers first in everything I do. Whether personally responding to customer inquiries or actively seeking feedback, I want my team to see that I'm committed to walking the talk.

However, it's not just about what I do; it's also about what I say. I make sure to consistently communicate our customer-centric values and expectations to the entire team. I share success stories highlighting the impact of putting customers at the center of our business and encouraging others to do the same.

Another crucial aspect of leadership in this context is providing the necessary support and resources. I understand that creating a customer-centric culture requires more than just lip service; it requires investment. That means providing training and development opportunities that empower our team to deliver exceptional customer experiences. It means investing in technology and tools that streamline processes and make it easier for us to serve our customers effectively.

Ultimately, leadership's role in creating a customer-centric culture is about setting the vision, modeling the behavior, and providing the support needed to bring that vision to life. It's about creating an environment where every team member feels empowered to go above and beyond for our customers because they know that's what we value most.

When it comes to running a successful business, one of the key lessons I've learned is the importance of keeping our customers at the forefront of everything we do. It's not enough to just say we prioritize their needs; we have to actively demonstrate it through our actions and decisions.

One strategy I've found incredibly effective is aligning our organizational goals with the needs and expectations of our customers. This means taking the time to truly understand who our customers are, what they value, and what challenges they face. By gaining this insight, we can tailor our products, services, and processes to better meet their needs.

For example, if we notice a recurring issue or pain point that our customers are experiencing, we prioritize addressing it. Whether it's streamlining our checkout process to make it more user-friendly or introducing new features based on customer feedback, we're constantly looking for ways to enhance the customer experience.

But it's not just about making changes based on customer feedback; it's also about leading by example. As the leader of the organization, I know that my actions speak louder than words. That's why I make it a point to embody a customer-centric mindset in everything I do.

Whether it's personally responding to customer inquiries or going above and beyond to resolve a problem, I want my team to see that prioritizing our customers isn't just a slogan; it's a way of life. I encourage my employees to do the same, emphasizing the importance of empathy, communication, and going the extra mile to ensure our customers feel valued and heard.

By leading by example and fostering a customer-centric mindset among our employees, we can create a culture where putting the customer first isn't just a goal; it's ingrained in our DNA. And when everyone in the organization is aligned around this common goal, it's amazing what we can achieve together.

Empowering Employees to Prioritize Customer Needs

In my experience leading a business, I've come to understand that one of the most effective ways to cultivate a customer-centric culture is by empowering my employees to prioritize the needs of our customers. This means instilling in them a genuine sense of empathy and understanding toward the people we serve.

One technique I've found to be particularly powerful is fostering open communication and dialogue among my team members. By encouraging them to actively listen to customer feedback and engage in meaningful conversations, we're able to gain valuable insights into their needs and concerns. This helps us better understand our customers and allows our employees to develop a deeper sense of empathy toward them.

Another technique I use is providing ongoing training and development opportunities focused on customer service skills. Whether it's through workshops, seminars, or online courses, I'm committed to equipping my team with the tools and knowledge they need to excel in their roles. This includes teaching them how to effectively communicate with customers, handle difficult situations with grace and professionalism, and anticipate their needs before they arise.

Additionally, I make it a point to recognize and reward employees who go above and beyond to deliver exceptional customer service. Whether it's a simple thank you or a more tangible reward such as a bonus or extra time off, I want my team to know that their efforts are valued and appreciated.

By empowering my employees to prioritize customer needs, I've seen firsthand the positive impact it can have on our business. Not only does it lead to happier and more satisfied customers, but it also fosters a sense of pride and ownership among my team members. And when everyone is working together toward a common goal, there's no limit to what we can achieve.

In my role as a business owner, I've recognized the importance of equipping my team with the necessary skills to cultivate a customer-centric approach. That's why I've invested in comprehensive training programs and resources designed to develop these essential skills among my employees.

First and foremost, I ensure that all new hires undergo thorough onboarding that includes training on customer service fundamentals. This initial training covers topics such as effective communication, active listening, and problem-solving techniques. By laying down this foundation from the start, I set the stage for a customer-focused mindset to flourish within my team.

In addition to initial training, I provide ongoing professional development opportunities focused specifically on customer-centric skills. This includes workshops, seminars, and online courses tailored to various aspects of customer service. These resources cover a range of topics, from handling customer inquiries to managing difficult situations with empathy and professionalism.

I also encourage my team members to seek external training programs and certifications to enhance their customer-centric skills. Whether it's attending industry conferences or enrolling in specialized courses, I believe in supporting my employees' continuous growth and development.

Furthermore, I've created internal resources such as knowledge databases and best practice guides to serve as reference materials for my team. These resources provide valuable insights and practical tips for delivering exceptional customer service across different touchpoints.

By investing in training programs and resources to develop customer-centric skills, I empower my team to excel in their roles and deliver outstanding customer experiences. This strengthens our relationships with clients and contributes to our business's overall success and growth.

As a business owner, I've realized that empowering my team with autonomy and decision-making authority is crucial for delivering exceptional customer service. Instead of micromanaging every interaction, I encourage my employees to take ownership of customer inquiries and provide solutions that best meet their needs.

By empowering my team in this way, I've observed a significant improvement in our ability to serve customers effectively. Rather than waiting for approval or guidance from higher-ups, my employees feel empowered to make decisions on the spot, leading to quicker resolutions and increased customer satisfaction.

I've implemented clear guidelines and frameworks within our organization to foster autonomy. These guidelines outline the boundaries within which employees can exercise their discretion and make decisions autonomously. By providing this framework, I ensure that my team feels confident in their ability to act in the customer's best interest without fear of overstepping their bounds.

In addition to autonomy, I also encourage a culture of continuous learning and improvement. This means providing ongoing training and development opportunities to enhance my team's skills and knowledge. By investing in their growth, I equip them with the tools they need to make informed decisions and deliver exceptional service consistently.

Furthermore, I make it a point to recognize and celebrate instances where employees demonstrate autonomy and make decisions that positively impact our customers. This reinforces the importance of autonomy and motivates others to follow suit.

By encouraging autonomy and decision-making authority within my team, I've seen firsthand how it leads to better customer outcomes and contributes to our business's overall success.

Integrating Customer Feedback into Organizational Processes

As a business owner, I've come to understand the immense value of integrating customer feedback into our organizational processes. It's like having a direct line to our customers' thoughts and feelings, allowing us to tailor our products and services to better meet their needs.

One of the methods we use to collect customer feedback is through surveys. We send surveys after customer interactions, asking them to rate their experience and provide additional comments or suggestions. These surveys help us gauge customer satisfaction and identify areas for improvement.

Another valuable source of feedback for us is online reviews. Whether on social media, review sites, or our website, we pay close attention to what customers say about us online. Positive reviews give us insight into what we're doing well, while negative reviews highlight areas where we need to make changes.

In addition to these methods, we also encourage direct communication with customers. We have channels in place, such as email and live chat, where customers can reach out to us with any questions or concerns. By being accessible and responsive, we show our customers that their feedback is important to us.

Once we've collected feedback, we will analyze it and extract actionable insights. We look for patterns and trends in the feedback, identifying common pain points or areas of delight. This information then informs our decision-making process, guiding us in making changes that will have the biggest impact on customer satisfaction.

Overall, integrating customer feedback into our organizational processes is essential for maintaining a customer-centric approach. It allows us to continuously improve and evolve, ensuring that we're always delivering the best possible experience for our customers.

In our business, we've learned that customer insights are like gold dust. They're the key to unlocking new opportunities and improving our products and services. One strategy we use is to directly incorporate customer feedback into our product development process. When customers provide suggestions or highlight areas for improvement, we take those insights seriously. For example, if we receive multiple requests for a certain feature, we'll prioritize adding it to our roadmap. This way, we're not just guessing what our customers want – we're actually listening to them and responding accordingly.

Another strategy is to regularly review customer feedback as a team. We hold meetings where we discuss the feedback we've received and brainstorm ideas for addressing any issues or concerns. This collaborative approach ensures that everyone in the company is aligned on our goals and priorities.

However, it's not enough to collect feedback; we must act on it. That's where the feedback loop comes in. By closing the loop with customers, we show them that their input is valued and that we're committed to improving based on their suggestions. Whether it's sending a follow-up email to let them know their feedback has been implemented or reaching out personally to thank them for their input, closing the loop is an essential part of the process.

Overall, incorporating customer insights into our decision-making processes is crucial for staying competitive in today's market. By listening to our customers and acting on their feedback, we're able to continuously learn and adapt, ensuring that we're always meeting – and hopefully exceeding – their expectations.

Aligning Processes and Systems with Customer-Centric Goals

In our company, we've always strived to put our customers at the center of everything we do. However, we realized that it's not just about saying it; it's about ensuring our processes and systems reflect that commitment. Therefore, we looked closely at our existing workflows and systems to see if they aligned with our customer-centric goals.

What we found was eye-opening. While some of our processes were designed with the customer in mind, others were more focused on internal efficiency or convenience. For example, our returns process was streamlined for us, but it wasn't necessarily the most customer-friendly experience. Customers had to jump through hoops to return a product, which didn't align with our goal of making their lives easier.

So, we set out to make some changes. We started by gathering feedback from our customers about their pain points with our current processes. We then looked at each process individually to identify areas where we could improve the customer experience.

One area we focused on was our customer service system. We realized that our current system made it difficult for customers to get the help they needed quickly and efficiently. So, we invested in a new customer service platform that streamlined the support process and made it easier for customers to reach us.

Another area we looked at was our order fulfillment process. Our current system was prone to errors, leading to delays and frustration for our customers. To address this, we implemented new quality control measures and invested in technology to automate certain aspects of the process.

Overall, aligning our processes and systems with our customer-centric goals has been a game-changer for our business. Not only have we seen an improvement in customer satisfaction, but we've also seen a positive impact on our bottom line. It just goes to show that when you put the customer first, everyone wins.

As I evaluated our business operations, I realized there were areas where we could streamline processes to better meet our customers' needs. One technique we implemented was simplifying our order fulfillment process. Previously, it involved multiple steps and handoffs between departments, leading to delays and potential errors. We restructured the workflow to minimize unnecessary steps, automate routine tasks, and empower employees to make decisions without unnecessary bureaucracy.

Additionally, we recognized the importance of leveraging technology to enhance the customer experience. We invested in a new customer relationship management (CRM) system that allowed us to centralize customer data, track interactions across channels, and personalize communication. This helped us provide more tailored support and anticipate customer needs more effectively. Furthermore, we integrated chatbots into our website to provide instant assistance to customers and reduce response times.

By streamlining our operations and leveraging technology, we've been able to better serve our customers and improve their overall experience with our brand. It's a continuous process of refinement, but we're committed to staying agile and responsive to our customers' evolving needs.

Measuring and Monitoring Progress Toward Customer-Centricity

As I reflect on our journey toward becoming a more customer-centric organization, I realize the importance of having metrics in place to gauge our progress. These metrics serve as guideposts, helping us understand how well we're meeting our goals and where we need to improve.

One key metric we use is customer satisfaction scores (CSAT). This metric gives us direct feedback from our customers about their experience with our products and services. By regularly tracking CSAT scores, we can identify trends and areas for improvement. For example, if we notice a decline in satisfaction scores after implementing a new process or launching a new product, it prompts us to investigate further and make necessary adjustments.

Another metric we pay close attention to is the customer retention rate. This tells us how many customers continue to do business with us over time. A high retention rate indicates that we're doing a good job of meeting our customer's needs and keeping them satisfied. On the other hand, a declining retention rate signals potential issues that need to be addressed, such as poor customer service or product quality.

In addition to these metrics, we also track key performance indicators (KPIs) related to customer service, such as average response time and resolution rate. These metrics help us ensure that we're providing timely and effective support to our customers whenever they need assistance.

Overall, by regularly monitoring these metrics, we can measure our progress toward becoming more customer-centric and make data-driven decisions to continually improve our operations and better serve our customers.

As I reflect on our journey toward becoming more customer-centric, I realize the importance of having effective strategies in place to track our progress and identify areas for improvement. These strategies ensure that we stay focused on prioritizing our customers' needs and experiences.

One strategy we employ is setting clear and measurable goals related to customer satisfaction and service quality. By establishing specific targets, such as achieving a certain level of customer satisfaction or reducing response times, we have tangible benchmarks to work toward. Regularly monitoring our performance against these goals allows us to track our progress over time and pinpoint areas where we may be falling short.

Another key strategy is soliciting feedback from both customers and employees. Customer feedback provides valuable insights into their experiences with our products and services, allowing us to identify pain points and areas for improvement. Similarly, employee feedback offers valuable perspectives on internal processes and culture, helping us identify opportunities to better support our customers.

In addition to gathering feedback, we also utilize data analytics to track key metrics related to customer satisfaction and service delivery. By analyzing trends and patterns in the data, we can identify areas of strength and areas that may require attention. For example, if we notice a decline in customer satisfaction scores for a particular product or service, we can investigate further to understand the root cause and take corrective action.

Regular evaluation and adjustment are essential to maintaining a customer-centric culture. Markets and customer preferences are constantly evolving, so it's crucial that we adapt and evolve along with them. By regularly reviewing our processes, soliciting feedback, and analyzing data, we can ensure that we remain responsive to our customers' needs and continue to deliver exceptional experiences.

Cultivating a Customer-Centric Mindset Across the Organization

As I look across my organization, I see the importance of instilling a customer-centric mindset in every team member. It's not just about providing great products or services; it's about understanding our customers' needs and making sure every decision we make is in their best interest.

One way I've found to cultivate this mindset is by creating a shared vision and language around customer-centricity. We've developed a clear mission statement that emphasizes our commitment to putting customers first in everything we do. This mission statement serves as a guiding light for our organization, reminding us of our purpose and values.

In addition to our mission statement, we've also developed a common language around customer-centricity. This language helps us communicate more effectively with one another and ensures that everyone is on the same page when it comes to serving our customers. For example, we use phrases like "customer satisfaction" and "customer experience" regularly in our discussions, reinforcing the importance of these concepts in our work.

Furthermore, we actively promote a culture of empathy and understanding within our organization. We encourage team members to put themselves in our customers' shoes and think about how they would want to be treated in a similar situation. This fosters a sense of empathy and helps us better understand and anticipate our customers' needs.

Overall, creating a shared vision and language around customer-centricity has been instrumental in cultivating a customer-centric mindset across our organization. It aligns our teams around a common goal and ensures that everyone is working together to deliver exceptional experiences for our customers.

In my company, fostering collaboration across departments has become a cornerstone of our customer-centric approach. We've come to realize that to truly meet the diverse needs of our customers, we need to break down silos and work together seamlessly as a unified team.

Encouraging cross-departmental collaboration starts with fostering an environment where communication flows freely and ideas are welcomed from all corners of the organization. We've implemented regular meetings and brainstorming sessions where team members from different departments come together to discuss customer challenges and brainstorm solutions. These sessions have proven to be invaluable, as they bring fresh perspectives to the table and often lead to innovative ideas that benefit our customers.

Additionally, we've invested in technology that facilitates collaboration and communication across departments. Our project management tools allow team members to easily share updates and coordinate efforts, ensuring everyone is aligned on our customer-centric goals.

But collaboration isn't just about working together on projects; it's also about celebrating successes and recognizing individuals who embody our customer-centric values. We make a point to highlight and celebrate team members who go above and beyond to deliver exceptional customer experiences. Whether it's through shout-outs in team meetings or recognition programs, we ensure that their efforts don't go unnoticed.

By encouraging cross-departmental collaboration and celebrating successes, we've built a culture where every team member feels empowered to contribute to our customer-centric mission. It's not just a slogan or a buzzword; it's a way of life that permeates every aspect of our organization. And ultimately, it's what sets us apart and drives our success in the marketplace.

Conclusion: Sustaining a Customer-Centric Culture

As I wrap up this chapter on building a customer-centric culture, I'm reminded of the journey my company and I have taken to put our customers at the heart of everything we do. We've covered a lot of ground, exploring the significance of customer-centricity, the role of leadership, empowering employees, integrating customer feedback, aligning processes, measuring progress, and fostering collaboration. Each topic has brought us closer to understanding what it truly means to be customer-centric.

Reflecting on our discussions, it's clear that building a customer-centric culture isn't just about implementing a few strategies; it's about ingraining a mindset into the fabric of our organization. It's about making a conscious effort every day to prioritize the needs and experiences of our customers in every decision we make.

Throughout this chapter, we've seen how leadership plays a critical role in championing customer-centric values and how empowering employees can lead to better customer outcomes. We've explored the importance of integrating customer feedback into our processes and aligning our systems to better serve our customers.

But perhaps most importantly, we've learned that sustaining a customer-centric culture requires ongoing commitment and investment. It's not a one-time effort; it's a continuous journey of improvement and adaptation.

As I conclude this chapter, I want to reinforce the importance of building a customer-centric culture in today's business landscape. Customers have more choices than ever before, and their loyalty can't be taken for granted. By prioritizing their needs and experiences, we differentiate ourselves in the market and create lasting relationships that drive long-term success.

So, my fellow business owners and leaders, I urge you to prioritize customer-centricity in your organizations. Let's continue to invest in our customers' success and work tirelessly to build cultures where they feel valued, heard, and understood. Together, we can create businesses that thrive by putting our customers first.

6

IMPLEMENTING EFFECTIVE CUSTOMER FEEDBACK SYSTEMS

As I begin this chapter on implementing customer feedback systems, I want to lay the groundwork for what we'll discuss and why it matters. Customer feedback systems are essentially the mechanisms we implement to collect and utilize customer feedback. This feedback can come in many forms, from surveys and reviews to social media comments and direct interactions.

You might be wondering, *Why bother with all this feedback in the first place?* Well, let me tell you, it's crucial for our business's success. Customer feedback is like a compass guiding us in the right direction. It helps us understand what our customers like, what they don't like, and what they want more of. Without this valuable input, we'd be operating in the dark, making decisions based on assumptions rather than real data.

This chapter will dive into the strategies for implementing effective feedback systems. We'll explore how to design surveys that get responses, how to leverage customer reviews and testimonials, and how to tap into the power of social media for insights. By the end of it, you'll have a solid understanding of how to harness the power of customer feedback to drive growth and improvement in your business.

Understanding the Types of Customer Feedback

Understanding the different types of customer feedback is like having a toolbox with various tools for different jobs. Each type of feedback provides us with unique insights into our customers' experiences and preferences.

Firstly, we have surveys, which are like questionnaires, that we send out to gather structured feedback. Surveys allow us to ask specific questions and quantify responses, giving us clear data to analyze. This can be invaluable for understanding trends and identifying areas for improvement.

Next up, we have reviews. These can come in the form of online reviews on platforms like Yelp or Google or testimonials shared directly with us. Reviews provide candid customer opinions about their experiences with our products or services. They give us a glimpse into what customers love about our offerings and where we might be falling short.

Social media is another goldmine for customer feedback. Whether it's comments on our posts or direct messages from customers, social media provides real-time insights into how people are feeling about our brand. It's a great way to gauge sentiment and promptly address any issues or concerns.

And let's not forget about direct interactions with customers. These interactions can provide invaluable qualitative feedback through emails, phone calls, or face-to-face conversations. They allow us to hear directly from customers about their experiences and address any issues in real time.

By understanding the different types of customer feedback available to us, we can ensure we're casting a wide net and gathering insights from various sources. This comprehensive approach allows us to paint a complete picture of our customers' experiences and make informed decisions to better serve them.

In the realm of customer feedback, there's a distinction between two main types: solicited and unsolicited feedback. Let's break it down.

Solicited feedback is like when you ask someone for their opinion. It's proactive. We might send out surveys after a customer makes a purchase or visits our store or directly ask for feedback through emails or on our website. Essentially, we're inviting customers to share their thoughts with us. Solicited feedback is structured and intentional, making it easier to analyze and act upon.

On the other hand, unsolicited feedback is more like when someone volunteers their thoughts without being prompted. This could be through online reviews, social media comments, or even emails sent to us without any prior request. It's spontaneous and often comes directly from the customer's experience, making it incredibly authentic and valuable. While unsolicited feedback can be more challenging to manage because it's unstructured, it provides genuine insights into how customers perceive our products or services in real-world situations.

Now, when it comes to analyzing feedback, we need to consider both quantitative and qualitative aspects. Quantitative feedback is all about the numbers. It's the data-driven side of things, like ratings on a scale of one to ten or the percentage of customers who said they were satisfied with their experience. Quantitative feedback helps us spot trends and measure our performance objectively.

On the flip side, qualitative feedback is all about the stories and anecdotes. It's the open-ended responses in surveys or the detailed comments in online reviews. Qualitative feedback gives color and context to the numbers, helping us understand the why behind the what. It's where we uncover the nuances and emotions that drive customer perceptions.

Both feedback types are essential for a holistic understanding of our customers' experiences. By analyzing both quantitative and qualitative feedback, we can paint a complete picture of what our customers want and need, allowing us to make informed decisions and continuously improve our products and services.

Designing Customer Feedback Surveys

When it comes to gathering feedback from our customers, creating effective surveys is key. Let me share how I approach crafting clear and concise survey questions.

First off, clarity is paramount. Our customers are busy people, so we want to make sure they understand what we're asking them. That means avoiding jargon or complicated language and making our questions easy to understand. I aim for simplicity without sacrificing the depth of the feedback we seek.

Next, I focus on being specific. Vague or ambiguous questions can lead to vague or ambiguous answers, which aren't helpful for anyone. Instead, I aim to ask precise questions targeting the information we seek. For example, instead of asking, "How satisfied are you with our service?" I might ask, "On a scale of 1 to 5, how satisfied were you with the speed of our delivery?"

Another thing I keep in mind is to make sure our questions are relevant. We want to gather feedback that will help us improve, so I only include questions that are directly related to our products, services, or customer experience. It's about getting to the heart of what matters most to our customers.

Lastly, brevity is key. Nobody wants to spend hours filling out a survey, so I keep ours short and sweet. I only ask the most important questions and avoid unnecessary fluff. That way, our customers can provide valuable feedback without feeling overwhelmed or frustrated.

By following these principles and crafting clear, concise survey questions, we can gather the insights we need to continuously improve and better serve our customers. It's all about making it easy for them to share their thoughts and ensuring that we're asking the right questions to drive meaningful change.

When it comes to gathering feedback from our customers, choosing the right survey delivery methods is crucial. We want to ensure that our surveys reach our customers in a convenient and non-intrusive way. That's why I've explored various options, from email to website pop-ups, to find what works best for our audience.

Email surveys are a classic choice. They allow us to reach customers directly in their inbox, where they're likely to see and respond to our requests for feedback. Plus, we can personalize the surveys to some extent, making them feel more tailored to each recipient. However, we have to be mindful of not overwhelming our customers with too many emails, so we use this method sparingly and strategically.

Website pop-ups can be another effective way to gather feedback, especially for capturing feedback at the moment. For example, if a customer completes a purchase or interacts with a specific feature on our website, we can trigger a pop-up asking for their thoughts or rating their experience. This real-time feedback can provide valuable insights into what's working well and what areas need improvement.

Incorporating feedback scales and open-ended questions is another important aspect of designing effective surveys. Feedback scales, such as Likert scales, allow customers to rate their satisfaction on a scale, providing us with quantitative data that's easy to analyze. Meanwhile, open-ended questions allow customers to share their thoughts in their own words, providing deeper insights into their experiences and feelings.

By combining different survey delivery methods and incorporating a mix of feedback scales and open-ended questions, we can gather a comprehensive understanding of our customers' opinions and experiences. It's all about finding the right balance between convenience and depth to ensure that our feedback surveys are effective in helping us improve and better serve our customers.

Leveraging Customer Reviews and Testimonials

When it comes to showcasing the value of our products or services, there's nothing quite like the power of customer reviews and testimonials. These snippets of feedback straight from the mouths of our satisfied customers can be a game-changer in building trust and credibility with potential buyers.

Encouraging our customers to leave reviews and testimonials isn't just about boosting our ego; it's about giving them a platform to share their experiences and help others make informed decisions. We've found a few effective ways to encourage this feedback flow.

Firstly, we make sure to ask for reviews at the right time. This could be immediately after a successful purchase or after a customer has had a chance to experience the full benefits of our product or service. Timing is everything; we want to catch them while they're still riding high on that wave of satisfaction.

We also make it as easy as possible for customers to leave reviews. This means providing clear instructions and accessible platforms, whether it's through our website, email, or social media channels. By removing any barriers or complications, we increase the likelihood of them taking that extra step to share their thoughts.

Incentivizing reviews can also be useful, although we tread carefully here to ensure that the feedback remains genuine and unbiased. This might involve offering discounts or exclusive offers in exchange for leaving a review, but it's important to maintain transparency and integrity throughout the process.

Lastly, we express our gratitude to customers who do take the time to leave reviews or testimonials. A simple thank you goes a long way in showing appreciation for their contribution and encourages them to continue engaging with our brand in the future.

Overall, leveraging customer reviews and testimonials is a win-win situation. We gain valuable insights and social proof to strengthen our reputation, and our customers feel valued and heard, fostering a sense of loyalty and connection with our brand.

In today's digital age, online reviews have become integral to how customers evaluate businesses. As a business owner, I recognize the importance of monitoring and responding to these reviews to maintain a positive reputation and build trust with potential customers.

Monitoring online reviews means keeping a close eye on platforms like Google, Yelp, and social media channels where customers might leave feedback about their experiences with my business. I make it a point to regularly check these platforms to stay informed about what customers are saying.

Regarding responding to reviews, my approach is straightforward yet sincere. For positive reviews, I express my gratitude to the customer for taking the time to share their positive experience. I aim to personalize my responses and show genuine appreciation for their feedback. This acknowledges their effort and demonstrates to other potential customers that I value and care about their satisfaction.

On the flip side, negative reviews can be a bit trickier to handle. Instead of getting defensive or dismissive, I approach negative feedback with empathy and a willingness to understand the customer's concerns. I respond promptly and professionally, addressing any issues raised and offering solutions or compensation where appropriate. By publicly acknowledging and addressing negative feedback, I show my commitment to customer satisfaction and willingness to make things right.

When it comes to utilizing positive reviews for marketing and reputation management, I leverage them across various channels to showcase the positive experiences of satisfied customers. Whether it's featuring testimonials on my website, sharing glowing reviews on social media, or incorporating them into marketing materials, positive reviews serve as powerful endorsements of my business.

In summary, monitoring and responding to online reviews is essential to managing my business's reputation and fostering trust with customers. By staying engaged with positive and negative feedback and leveraging positive reviews for marketing purposes, I can continue to build a strong and positive reputation for my business.

Implementing Social Listening Strategies

As a business owner, staying attuned to what customers are saying about my products or services on social media is vital. Social media platforms like Facebook, Twitter, and Instagram provide valuable insights into customer sentiments, preferences, and experiences.

Monitoring social media for customer feedback involves regularly checking mentions, comments, and direct messages across these platforms. I keep a close eye on relevant hashtags, brand mentions, and comments on posts related to my business to ensure I don't miss any positive or negative feedback.

When I spot feedback on social media, I take prompt action to address it. Positive comments and compliments are acknowledged with gratitude and sometimes even shared to showcase customer satisfaction. For negative feedback or complaints, I respond swiftly and empathetically, aiming to resolve issues and turn negative experiences into positive ones.

In addition to reacting to direct mentions, I also pay attention to broader conversations about topics related to my industry or niche. By monitoring industry-related hashtags and participating in relevant discussions, I gain valuable insights into customer preferences, pain points, and emerging trends.

Implementing social listening strategies allows me to stay connected with my audience, understand their needs and concerns, and proactively engage with them to foster positive relationships. By leveraging social media as a feedback channel, I demonstrate my commitment to customer satisfaction and continuously improve the quality of my products or services.

Engaging with customers on social media platforms has become integral to my business strategy. Platforms like Facebook, Twitter, and Instagram offer unique opportunities to connect with my audience, address their concerns, and showcase my brand's personality.

I aim to be authentic and responsive when I engage with customers on social media. I actively participate in conversations by replying to comments, answering questions, and acknowledging both positive and negative feedback. Doing so demonstrates to my customers that their voices are heard and valued.

One of the most effective ways I engage with customers on social media is by sharing content that resonates with them. Whether it's educational articles, behind-the-scenes glimpses of my business, or user-generated content, I strive to create content that sparks meaningful interactions and encourages engagement.

In addition to engaging directly with customers, I also use social listening tools to track brand mentions and sentiment. These tools allow me to monitor conversations about my brand across various social media platforms in real time. By analyzing the tone and context of these mentions, I gain valuable insights into how my brand is perceived and can adjust my approach accordingly.

For example, if I notice a spike in negative sentiment around a particular product or service, I can quickly address the issue and prevent it from escalating. Conversely, if I receive positive feedback or praise, I can amplify it by sharing it with my audience and expressing gratitude.

Overall, engaging with customers on social media and utilizing social listening tools are essential components of my customer feedback strategy. By actively participating in conversations and monitoring brand mentions, I can better understand my customers' needs and preferences, ultimately driving growth and loyalty for my business.

Analyzing and Interpreting Customer Feedback Data

As a business owner, I understand the importance of collecting and organizing feedback data from my customers. This information is like a compass guiding me toward making informed decisions that benefit my business and customers.

When it comes to collecting feedback data, I have various channels in place to gather insights from my customers. Whether through surveys, reviews, social media interactions, or direct communication, I capture feedback from every possible touchpoint.

Once I have collected the feedback, my next step is to organize it in a way that allows me to extract meaningful insights. I categorize the data based on different criteria, such as the type of feedback, the product or service it relates to, and the sentiment expressed by the customer.

For instance, if I receive feedback about a specific product feature, I categorize it under that product's feedback section. Similarly, if a customer leaves a review expressing satisfaction or dissatisfaction, I categorize it accordingly to understand the overall sentiment.

Organizing feedback data not only helps me make sense of the information but also enables me to identify patterns and trends. By analyzing the data, I can uncover recurring issues, identify areas for improvement, and recognize aspects of my business that resonate well with customers.

Moreover, analyzing customer feedback data allows me to gain valuable insights into my customers' needs, preferences, and pain points. This understanding empowers me to tailor my products, services, and overall customer experience to better meet their expectations.

Collecting and organizing feedback data is not just about gathering information; it's about harnessing the power of customer insights to drive positive change and continuously improve my business.

In my business journey, I've learned that understanding customer feedback goes beyond just listening to individual comments or reviews. It's about spotting trends and patterns that emerge from the collective voices of our customers.

Identifying these trends and patterns is like connecting the dots in a puzzle. Each piece of feedback contributes to the bigger picture, revealing valuable insights about our products, services, and overall customer experience.

For example, let's say we notice a recurring theme in customer feedback about a particular product feature. Maybe several customers are expressing frustration with its functionality or suggesting enhancements. Recognizing this trend allows us to address the issue proactively, whether through product updates, additional support resources, or better communication about using the feature effectively.

Similarly, by analyzing feedback across different channels and touchpoints, we can identify broader patterns in customer sentiment. For instance, if we observe a spike in negative reviews following a recent website redesign, it signals a potential dissatisfaction with the changes. This insight prompts us to revisit our design choices and make adjustments based on customer preferences.

Once we've identified trends and patterns, the next step is to extract actionable insights from the data. This means distilling the feedback into clear takeaways that inform our decision-making and drive tangible improvements in our business operations.

For instance, if we notice a recurring complaint about slow response times to customer inquiries, we can implement measures to streamline our support processes and reduce wait times. If customers consistently praise a specific aspect of our service, we can capitalize on that strength and incorporate it into our marketing efforts to attract more customers.

Ultimately, the goal is to leverage customer feedback as a catalyst for positive change and continuous improvement. By identifying trends, extracting actionable insights, and taking decisive actions based on customer input, we can strengthen our business and enhance the overall customer experience.

Integrating Customer Feedback into Business Processes

In my business, I've found that customer feedback isn't just valuable for the customer service team—it's something that should be shared across all departments. Integrating feedback into our business processes becomes a driving force behind our decision-making and improvements.

For example, let's say our customer support team receives feedback about a recurring issue with a product feature. Instead of keeping this information isolated within the support department, we make it a point to share it with our product development team. By doing so, we ensure that everyone is aware of the challenges customers are facing and can work collaboratively to address them.

Sharing feedback insights across departments isn't just about pointing out problems—it's also about highlighting opportunities for innovation and enhancement. If customers consistently praise a certain aspect of our service, such as our user-friendly interface, we make sure to share that positive feedback with our marketing team. This allows them to leverage it in their campaigns and messaging to attract more customers.

Moreover, integrating customer feedback into our business processes fosters a culture of customer-centricity throughout the organization. When everyone—from sales and marketing to product development and operations—is aware of the feedback we receive from customers, it reinforces the importance of prioritizing their needs and experiences in everything we do.

We use various communication channels to facilitate this integration, such as regular team meetings, shared documents, and collaboration tools. By making feedback easily accessible to all employees, we ensure everyone has the opportunity to contribute to our ongoing efforts to improve and evolve as a business.

Overall, integrating customer feedback into our business processes isn't just a one-time task—it's an ongoing commitment to listening, learning, and adapting based on the insights we receive from our customers. By making feedback a central part of our decision-making and operations, we can continuously strive to meet and exceed customer expectations.

In my business, we firmly believe that customer feedback isn't just something to collect—it's something to act upon. When we receive feedback from our customers, whether it's about a product feature or their overall experience with our service, we take it seriously and use it to drive improvements.

One way we incorporate feedback into our operations is by integrating it into our product development process. For example, suppose we consistently receive feedback about a particular feature that customers find confusing or difficult to use. In that case, we make it a priority to address that in our next product update. We analyze the feedback to understand the root cause of the issue, brainstorm potential solutions, and then work with our development team to implement the necessary changes.

However, it's not just about fixing problems; it's also about seizing opportunities to enhance our products and services based on customer suggestions. If we receive feedback about a new feature idea or a specific improvement that customers would like to see, we carefully evaluate it to determine if it aligns with our overall product vision and goals. If it does, we explore ways to incorporate it into our roadmap and prioritize its development accordingly.

Implementing changes based on customer feedback isn't always easy, especially when it requires significant resources or shifts in our existing processes. However, we recognize that it's essential to improve the overall customer experience and maintain our competitive edge in the market. That's why we're committed to being agile and responsive to customer needs, even if it means making tough decisions or pivoting our strategy based on their feedback.

In the end, our goal is simple: to continuously evolve and refine our products and services to better meet the needs and expectations of our customers. By actively listening to their feedback and taking action to address their concerns and suggestions, we not only improve the customer experience but also build trust and loyalty that can drive long-term success for our business.

Continuous Improvement and Adaptation

In my business, I've come to realize that improvement isn't a one-time thing—it's an ongoing journey. That's why we've prioritized establishing a feedback loop that allows us to continuously learn and adapt based on the insights we gather from our customers.

Setting up this feedback loop was a bit of a process. At first, we started small, simply asking our customers for their thoughts and opinions after interacting with our products or services. We wanted to make it easy for them to share their feedback, so we provided multiple channels for them to do so, whether through email surveys, online forms, or even just a quick chat with our support team.

Once we started collecting feedback, the next step was to analyze it and identify any recurring themes or patterns. This wasn't always easy, especially when we were dealing with a large volume of feedback, but we knew it was essential for understanding our customers' needs and preferences.

As we analyzed the feedback, we noticed certain areas where we could improve. Maybe there was a feature that customers were consistently asking for, or perhaps there was a common pain point that we hadn't addressed adequately. Whatever the case, we made it a priority to take action based on what we learned.

However, it didn't stop there. We quickly realized that the feedback loop needed to be a continuous process, not just a one-off initiative. That's why we implemented systems and processes to ensure feedback was regularly collected, analyzed, and acted upon. Whether it was through regular surveys, ongoing customer interviews, or real-time monitoring of social media channels, we were always listening and learning.

As a result, we were able to adapt and evolve our products and services over time, making them even better suited to our customers' needs. But perhaps even more importantly, we demonstrated to our customers that we were listening to them and that their feedback truly mattered to us. That, in turn, helped to strengthen our relationships with them and build trust and loyalty that would endure over the long term.

As a business owner, keeping an eye on the effectiveness of our feedback systems is crucial. It's like checking our operation's pulse, ensuring we're staying healthy and responsive to our customers' needs.

We didn't just set up our feedback systems and then forget about them. Instead, we regularly monitored how well they were working. We looked at things like response rates to our surveys, the quality of the feedback we were receiving, and how quickly we could implement changes based on that feedback.

We didn't hesitate to make improvements if we noticed any areas where our feedback systems were falling short. Maybe we needed to tweak the wording of our survey questions to make them clearer, or perhaps we needed to offer additional incentives to encourage more customers to participate. Whatever the case, we were always looking for ways to fine-tune our approach and make our feedback systems as effective as possible.

But it wasn't just about the mechanics of our feedback systems. We also worked hard to cultivate a culture of continuous improvement and customer-centricity within our organization. We wanted every member of our team to understand the importance of listening to our customers and using their feedback to drive positive change.

To foster this culture, we provided training and resources to help our employees develop the skills they needed to gather and analyze feedback effectively. We also encouraged open communication and collaboration across departments so everyone felt empowered to contribute to the feedback process.

Perhaps most importantly, we led by example. We made it clear through our actions that listening to our customers and constantly striving to improve were non-negotiable values for our business. And over time, that commitment to continuous improvement became ingrained in our company culture, driving us to always be looking for ways to better serve our customers.

Conclusion: Maximizing the Value of Customer Feedback

As we wrap up this chapter, I want to take a moment to summarize what we've covered and emphasize the importance of implementing effective feedback systems in our businesses.

Throughout this chapter, we've explored various strategies for gathering and leveraging customer feedback. From designing clear and concise surveys to monitoring social media channels for insights, we've seen how valuable feedback can be in guiding our decision-making and improving the customer experience.

We've also discussed the significance of analyzing feedback data to identify trends and patterns and the importance of integrating feedback into our business processes to drive meaningful change.

However, gathering feedback is only the first step. We must act based on what we learn to maximize its value. That means improving our products, services, and processes based on the insights we gather from our customers.

In conclusion, I want to encourage all organizations to prioritize customer feedback and use it as a catalyst for growth and improvement. By listening to our customers and acting on their feedback, we can build stronger, more successful businesses that meet the needs of those we serve.

7
LEVERAGING TECHNOLOGY FOR MULTICHANNEL SUPPORT

Providing excellent customer support is crucial for success in today's business landscape. As a business owner, I understand the importance of being available to customers through various channels. This is where multichannel support comes into play.

Multichannel support refers to the practice of offering assistance to customers through different communication channels such as phone, email, chat, social media, and more. It's about meeting customers where they are and providing them with the support they need, regardless of the platform they choose to reach out on.

The significance of multichannel support cannot be overstated. In a world where customers expect instant gratification and seamless experiences, offering support across multiple channels is essential for staying competitive. It allows businesses to cater to their customer base's diverse preferences and needs, ultimately enhancing customer satisfaction and loyalty.

In this chapter, we'll explore how leveraging technology can help us deliver effective multichannel support. We'll delve into various tools and software solutions designed to streamline customer interactions across different channels. By the end of this chapter, you'll have a clear understanding of how technology can elevate your multichannel support efforts and help you better serve your customers.

Understanding Multichannel Communication

As a business owner, I've come to recognize the importance of understanding multichannel communication. It's not just about having a phone number or an email address for customers to contact us. It's about being present across various channels where our customers are active.

Firstly, let's break down what multichannel communication means. It encompasses a range of channels through which customers can interact with our business, such as phone calls, emails, live chat on our website, social media platforms like Facebook and Twitter, and even messaging apps like WhatsApp or Facebook Messenger.

The reason why offering support across multiple channels is so crucial is simple: customers have different preferences when it comes to communication. Some might prefer the convenience of sending an email, while others may opt for the immediacy of a phone call or a chat message. By being available on all these channels, we're meeting our customers where they feel most comfortable, making it easier for them to reach out to us with their questions or concerns.

Of course, with the benefits of multichannel communication also come challenges. Managing inquiries from different channels can be daunting, and it requires careful coordination to ensure that each customer receives a consistent and satisfactory experience, regardless of the channel they use to contact us.

However, despite these challenges, the benefits of multichannel communication far outweigh the drawbacks. By offering support across multiple channels, we're not only improving customer satisfaction and loyalty, but we're also positioning ourselves as a modern and customer-centric business committed to meeting our clientele's diverse needs.

Implementing Multichannel Support Technology

As a business owner, I've had to navigate the complex world of customer support technology, especially when it comes to managing support across multiple channels. Let me share some insights into implementing multichannel support technology.

When it comes to managing support across various channels like phone, email, chat, and social media, having the right technology in place is crucial. These tools streamline communication, help track interactions, and ensure a consistent experience for our customers.

One of the first steps in implementing multichannel support technology is to assess our needs and find the right solution that fits our business. There are many options available, ranging from all-in-one customer support platforms to specialized tools for specific channels.

Once we've selected the appropriate technology, the next step is implementation. This involves setting up the software, configuring it to meet our requirements, and integrating it with our existing systems. Depending on the complexity of the solution, this process may require some time and effort, but it's essential to get it right to ensure smooth operations.

Training our team is another crucial aspect of implementing multichannel support technology. We need to ensure that everyone is familiar with the new tools and understands how to use them effectively. This might involve providing training sessions or access to tutorials and resources to help our team get up to speed.

Finally, ongoing monitoring and optimization are essential. We should regularly review our technology usage, gather customer and employee feedback, and adjust as needed to improve efficiency and effectiveness.

Implementing the right multichannel support technology can streamline our customer support operations, enhance the customer experience, and ultimately drive business growth.

In my journey as a business owner, I've come to realize the importance of choosing the right software platforms and tools to manage multichannel support effectively. With so many options available, deciding which is the best fit for my business can be overwhelming.

To make an informed decision, I've taken the time to compare different software platforms and tools. This involves researching and evaluating each option's features, functionality, pricing, and user reviews. By carefully considering these factors, I can identify the solution that aligns most closely with my business needs and budget.

Once I've selected a software platform, the next step is to integrate and optimize it within my existing systems and processes. Integration is key to ensuring seamless communication and data flow between different channels and departments. This might involve customizing workflows, setting up automation rules, and syncing customer data across platforms.

Optimizing multichannel support systems requires ongoing monitoring and adjustment. I regularly assess performance metrics, such as response times, resolution rates, and customer satisfaction scores, to identify areas for improvement. I can fine-tune my support processes and workflows by analyzing this data to enhance efficiency and effectiveness.

In addition to optimizing individual channels, I also focus on creating a unified experience for customers across all touchpoints. This involves ensuring consistency in branding, messaging, and service quality, regardless of the channel they choose to engage with us on.

By carefully comparing software platforms, integrating them effectively, and continuously optimizing my multi-channel support systems, I can deliver exceptional customer experiences and drive business success.

Managing Customer Interactions Across Channels

Ensuring consistency and coherence in messaging is paramount in managing customer interactions across various channels. Picture this: a customer reaches out to us on social media with a question about our product. Meanwhile, another customer sends an email seeking assistance with a similar issue. Both interactions present opportunities to provide helpful and consistent responses.

I've implemented techniques to streamline our messaging across channels to achieve this. First and foremost, I've established clear guidelines and communication standards for our team members to follow. These guidelines outline the tone, language, and key messaging points to maintain consistency in our interactions.

Furthermore, I prioritize regular training and coaching sessions to reinforce these standards and ensure that every team member understands the importance of consistent messaging. By equipping our team with the necessary knowledge and skills, we can confidently engage with customers across various channels while maintaining a cohesive brand voice.

Additionally, I leverage technology to support our efforts in managing customer interactions. Using customer relationship management (CRM) software, we can track and review past interactions with customers to ensure that our messaging remains consistent over time. This allows us to provide personalized and contextually relevant responses, regardless of the channel used by the customer.

Active monitoring and feedback are another important aspect of managing customer interactions across channels. We regularly review customer interactions to identify any inconsistencies or areas for improvement. By soliciting feedback from customers and team members alike, we can continuously refine our messaging strategies to better meet the needs and expectations of our audience.

Implementing these techniques and strategies ensures that our messaging remains consistent and coherent across all channels. This not only enhances the customer experience but also strengthens our brand identity and fosters trust and loyalty among our customers.

Training and empowering our support agents to effectively handle multichannel interactions is crucial in ensuring a seamless and satisfactory experience for our customers. Imagine this scenario: a customer contacts us via email with a question about our services, while another reaches out through our live chat feature seeking assistance with a technical issue. Both interactions demand prompt and knowledgeable responses, regardless of the channel used.

I prioritize comprehensive training programs to equip our support agents with the skills and confidence needed to navigate multichannel interactions. These programs cover various aspects, including communication techniques, problem-solving strategies, and familiarity with our products and services. By providing our team with the necessary knowledge and tools, we empower them to effectively address customer inquiries and concerns across different channels.

Moreover, I emphasize the importance of adaptability and flexibility in handling multichannel interactions. Each communication channel has unique challenges and nuances, and our support agents must be equipped to navigate them seamlessly. Through role-playing exercises and real-life scenarios, we simulate various multichannel interactions to help our team members develop the skills to respond appropriately.

In addition to training, I encourage autonomy and decision-making among our support agents. Empowering them to make informed decisions enables them to provide personalized and timely assistance to our customers, regardless of the channel used. By trusting our team members to handle multichannel interactions independently, we foster a sense of ownership and accountability, which ultimately contributes to a better customer experience.

Maintaining a unified customer experience across all channels is paramount to our success. Whether a customer reaches out to us via email, phone, chat, or social media, they should receive consistent and cohesive support. This consistency enhances customer satisfaction, strengthens our brand reputation, and fosters long-term loyalty. By prioritizing training and empowerment and emphasizing the importance of a unified customer experience, we can continue to excel in our multichannel support efforts.

Leveraging Data and Analytics in Multichannel Support

In our pursuit of delivering top-notch customer support across multiple channels, harnessing the power of data and analytics has become a cornerstone of our strategy. Picture this: a customer reaches out to us via email, while another prefers to engage through our social media platforms. Each interaction presents a unique opportunity to gather valuable insights into our customers' preferences, needs, and pain points.

By leveraging data analytics, we can track and analyze customer interactions across all channels effectively. We utilize advanced analytics tools to collect data on various metrics, such as response times, resolution rates, and customer satisfaction scores. This data allows us to gain a comprehensive understanding of how our customers engage with us across different channels, enabling us to identify areas for improvement and optimization.

Extracting insights from customer data is where the real magic happens. We can uncover valuable patterns, trends, and correlations hidden within the data through careful analysis. For example, we may discover that customers who contact us via chat tend to have higher satisfaction levels than those who contact us via email. Armed with this knowledge, we can allocate resources more efficiently, prioritize certain channels, and tailor our support strategies to meet our customers' needs better.

Moreover, data analytics empowers us to continuously refine and enhance our support processes and performance. By identifying bottlenecks, streamlining workflows, and implementing targeted interventions, we can improve our support operations' overall efficiency and effectiveness. For instance, if we notice a recurring issue across multiple channels, we can proactively address it to prevent future occurrences and ensure a smoother customer experience.

Data and analytics serve as our compass, guiding us toward greater customer satisfaction and operational excellence. By harnessing the power of data-driven insights, we can make informed decisions, optimize our multichannel support efforts, and ultimately deliver a superior experience to our valued customers.

In our journey to enhance our customer support capabilities, we've embarked on a fascinating exploration of AI and machine learning technologies. These cutting-edge tools have revolutionized the way we interact with our customers, allowing us to provide predictive support and deliver personalized experiences like never before.

Let me paint a picture of how this works. Imagine a scenario where a customer contacts us with a specific issue. With AI-powered predictive support, our systems can analyze past interactions, customer data, and contextual information to anticipate the customer's needs before they even articulate them. For example, suppose a customer mentions a problem with their product. In that case, our AI system can predict potential solutions based on similar cases in the past, saving time and effort for both the customer and our support team.

But it doesn't stop there. With machine learning algorithms continuously analyzing vast amounts of data, we can create highly personalized customer experiences. By understanding their preferences, behaviors, and history with our brand, we can tailor our responses, recommendations, and offers to meet their individual needs. For instance, if a customer frequently purchases a particular product, our system can suggest complementary products or offer exclusive discounts tailored to their interests.

Implementing AI and machine learning technologies into our support processes has been a game-changer for us. Not only does it enable us to provide faster and more accurate assistance to our customers, but it also allows us to forge deeper connections and foster loyalty through personalized interactions. By leveraging the power of these advanced technologies, we're not just resolving issues – we're creating memorable experiences that leave a lasting impression on our customers.

Enhancing Security and Privacy in Multichannel Support

As we continue to expand our multichannel support capabilities, ensuring the security and privacy of our customers' data remains a top priority. In today's digital landscape, where cyber threats lurk around every corner, safeguarding sensitive information has never been more critical.

Let's talk about cybersecurity risks. With multiple communication channels in play – from phone calls and emails to social media and live chat – the potential for data breaches and cyber-attacks is heightened. Hackers are constantly devising new tactics to exploit vulnerabilities and gain unauthorized access to confidential information, putting both our customers and our business at risk.

To counter these threats, we've implemented robust protocols and measures designed to fortify our defenses and protect customer data across all channels. This includes encryption technologies to secure communications, stringent authentication processes to verify the identity of users, and regular security audits to identify and address any vulnerabilities proactively.

But security isn't just about technology – it's also about instilling a culture of vigilance and accountability within our organization. We provide ongoing training and education to our staff to ensure they understand the importance of cybersecurity and are equipped to recognize and respond to potential threats effectively.

By taking a proactive approach to security and privacy in our multichannel support operations, we're safeguarding our customers' trust and confidence as well as the reputation and integrity of our business. It's a responsibility we don't take lightly and one that we're committed to upholding as we continue navigating the ever-evolving digital communication landscape.

Ensuring compliance with privacy regulations like GDPR and CCPA is a cornerstone of our multichannel support practices. These regulations are in place to safeguard personal data and impose strict guidelines on how businesses handle and protect that information.

Adhering to these regulations isn't just a legal obligation; it's a commitment to our customers' privacy and trust. We understand the importance of respecting their personal information and take proactive steps to ensure it's handled with the utmost care and integrity across all our support channels.

To achieve compliance, we've implemented a comprehensive framework that aligns with the requirements outlined in GDPR and CCPA. This includes:

1. Transparency: We're transparent with our customers about how their data is collected, used, and shared. We provide clear and easily accessible privacy notices that outline our data practices in simple, understandable language.

2. Consent: We obtain explicit customer consent before collecting or processing their personal data. This ensures that they have control over how their information is used and allows them to opt out if they choose.

3. Data Minimization: We only collect and retain the minimum amount of data necessary to fulfill our support obligations. This helps minimize the risk of data breaches and ensures that we're not storing more information than we need.

4. Security Measures: We've implemented robust security measures to protect customer data from unauthorized access, disclosure, alteration, or destruction. This includes encryption, access controls, and regular security audits to identify and address vulnerabilities.

5. Compliance Monitoring: We continuously monitor our multichannel support practices to ensure ongoing

compliance with GDPR, CCPA, and other relevant privacy regulations. This includes conducting regular assessments, updating our policies and procedures as needed, and providing ongoing training to our staff.

By prioritizing compliance with privacy regulations, we're meeting our legal obligations and demonstrating our commitment to earning and maintaining our customers' trust. We recognize that their privacy is paramount, and we're dedicated to upholding the highest standards of data protection in all our interactions.

Optimizing Multichannel Support for Mobile Devices

In today's fast-paced digital world, ensuring that our support solutions are mobile-friendly is essential. With more and more people relying on their smartphones and tablets to access information and communicate, having a mobile-friendly support system is no longer just a convenience – it's a necessity.

The importance of mobile-friendly support solutions stems from mobile devices becoming ubiquitous in our daily lives. Whether it's checking emails, browsing social media, or shopping online, people are increasingly turning to their mobile devices to meet their needs. As a business owner, it's crucial for me to recognize this trend and adapt our support strategies accordingly.

One of the key reasons why mobile-friendly support is so important is accessibility. With mobile devices, customers can reach out for support anytime, anywhere – whether they're at home, on the go, or even traveling. By providing support solutions that are optimized for mobile, we're making it easier for customers to get the assistance they need whenever they need it.

Another reason why mobile-friendly support is essential is user experience. Mobile devices have smaller screens and different interaction patterns compared to desktop computers, so it's important that our support solutions are tailored to these devices. This means optimizing our websites, apps, and communication channels for mobile use, ensuring they're easy to navigate, responsive, and user-friendly.

Furthermore, mobile-friendly support solutions can also improve customer satisfaction and loyalty. When customers can easily access support on their mobile devices, they're more likely to have a positive experience with our brand. This can lead to increased customer satisfaction, repeat business, and positive word-of-mouth referrals.

In summary, optimizing our support solutions for mobile devices is crucial in today's digital landscape. By recognizing the importance of mobile accessibility, prioritizing user experience, and embracing mobile-friendly technologies, we can ensure that our customers have a seamless and satisfying support experience, regardless of their device.

As a business owner, ensuring that our support channels are optimized for mobile devices is a top priority. With more and more customers relying on their smartphones and tablets to engage with our brand, it's essential that we provide a seamless and efficient support experience across all devices.

To achieve this, we've implemented several strategies to optimize our support channels for mobile devices. One of the key strategies is ensuring that our website and online platforms are mobile-responsive. This means that regardless of the device customers are using – whether it's a smartphone, tablet, or desktop computer – they can easily access and navigate our support resources without any hassle. By adopting a responsive design approach, we're able to provide a consistent and user-friendly experience across all devices, ensuring that customers can find the information they need quickly and easily.

In addition to optimizing our website, we've also developed a mobile app to complement our online support channels. Our mobile app allows customers to access support resources, submit inquiries, and engage with our brand directly from their smartphones. By offering a dedicated mobile app, we can provide customers with a convenient and streamlined support experience tailored specifically to their mobile devices.

Furthermore, we've incorporated responsive design principles into our communication channels, such as email and live chat. This ensures that customers can easily reach out for support and receive timely assistance, regardless of their device. By embracing responsive design across all our support channels, we're able to deliver a cohesive and seamless multichannel support experience that meets the needs of our mobile customers.

Optimizing our support channels for mobile devices is essential for providing a superior customer experience in today's digital age. By incorporating responsive design principles, developing a dedicated mobile app, and ensuring consistency across all our communication channels, we can deliver a seamless and efficient support experience accessible to customers wherever they are.

Addressing Challenges and Overcoming Obstacles

In the business world, every new initiative comes with its own challenges and obstacles, and implementing multichannel support is no exception. As a business owner, it's crucial to identify these challenges and develop strategies to overcome them to ensure the success of our multichannel support efforts.

One common challenge we face in implementing multichannel support is the complexity of managing multiple communication channels. With phone support, email, live chat, social media, and other channels all in play, it can be overwhelming to keep track of customer inquiries and ensure timely responses across each platform. This complexity can lead to inefficiencies and communication gaps if not managed effectively.

Another challenge is maintaining consistency and coherence in messaging across all channels. Each communication channel may have its own tone, style, and set of guidelines, making it challenging to ensure a unified brand voice and messaging strategy. Inconsistencies in messaging can confuse customers and erode trust in our brand, so addressing this challenge head-on is essential.

Additionally, ensuring data security and privacy across multiple channels is a significant concern. With sensitive customer information being shared across various platforms, there's a risk of data breaches and privacy violations if proper security measures aren't in place. Compliance with regulations such as GDPR and CCPA adds another layer of complexity to this challenge.

Finally, another obstacle we encounter is the need for ongoing training and support for our team members. With new technologies and communication channels constantly emerging, it's essential to keep our support agents up to date with the latest tools and best practices. Without adequate training and support, our team may struggle to effectively handle multichannel interactions and provide the level of service our customers expect.

Despite these challenges, I'm confident that we can overcome any obstacles and successfully implement multichannel support with careful planning, strategic decision-making, and a commitment to continuous improvement. By addressing these challenges head-on and leveraging technology and data analytics to our advantage, we can provide our customers with the exceptional support they deserve across all channels.

MASTERING CUSTOMER SUPPORT

In the realm of multichannel support, navigating through obstacles and fine-tuning processes to ensure seamless customer experiences is a continual journey. As a business owner, I've found that employing strategic strategies can help overcome barriers and optimize multichannel support processes for maximum effectiveness.

One approach we've adopted is to streamline our support workflows by leveraging automation and technology. By integrating chatbots and automated response systems, we can efficiently handle routine inquiries, freeing up our human agents to focus on more complex issues that require personalized attention. This improves efficiency and enhances the overall customer experience by reducing wait times and ensuring swift resolutions.

Another strategy we've found effective is to prioritize consistency and coherence across all communication channels. We've established clear guidelines and brand standards for our support team to follow, ensuring our messaging remains consistent regardless of the channel used. Whether a customer reaches out via email, phone, or social media, they can expect a cohesive and unified experience that reflects our brand values and identity.

Furthermore, we actively solicit feedback from our customers to identify pain points and areas for improvement in our multichannel support processes. We can continuously refine our approach and adapt to their evolving needs and preferences by listening to their insights and incorporating their suggestions. This customer-centric approach fosters stronger relationships with our customers and drives innovation and growth within our organization.

As for case studies and examples of successful multichannel support implementations, one standout example is a software company that seamlessly integrated live chat support into its mobile app. By offering real-time assistance directly within the app, they could provide immediate solutions to customer queries and technical issues, resulting in higher customer satisfaction and retention rates. Another example is a retail brand that leveraged social media channels to proactively engage with customers and address their concerns in a timely manner. By actively monitoring and responding to customer feedback on platforms like Twitter and Facebook, they were able to turn potentially negative experiences into positive ones and build stronger brand loyalty.

Overall, by employing strategic strategies, prioritizing consistency and coherence, and actively seeking customer feedback, businesses can overcome barriers and optimize their multichannel support processes to deliver exceptional customer experiences.

Conclusion: Embracing Multichannel Support for Customer Success

As I wrap up this chapter on multichannel support, it's essential to highlight the key takeaways and strategies that we've explored. Throughout our discussion, we've delved into the significance of leveraging technology to enhance customer support across various channels, from phone calls to social media platforms.

We've seen how offering support across multiple channels is not just a convenience but a necessity in today's digital landscape. Customers expect to interact with businesses through their preferred channels, whether it's via email, chat, or social media. By embracing multichannel support, organizations can meet these expectations and provide a seamless and cohesive experience across all touchpoints.

One of the recurring themes we've touched upon is the importance of technology in facilitating effective multichannel support. Technology plays a crucial role in streamlining support processes, improving response times, and ultimately enhancing customer satisfaction, from sophisticated software platforms to AI-powered chatbots.

As we conclude this chapter, I want to reinforce the significance of prioritizing multichannel support to drive customer success. By investing in the right technology and implementing strategic strategies, organizations can not only meet but exceed customer expectations, fostering loyalty and long-term relationships.

I urge fellow business owners and leaders to embrace multichannel support as a core component of their customer service strategy. By doing so, we can create meaningful connections with our customers, build trust, and ultimately drive business growth and success. Let's commit to prioritizing multichannel support and harnessing the power of technology to deliver exceptional experiences to our valued customers.

CONCLUSION: THE PATH TO EXCEPTIONAL CUSTOMER SUPPORT

As I reflect on the insights and strategies we've uncovered throughout our journey, it's clear that customer support is the cornerstone of business success. Throughout the chapters, we've explored various facets of providing exceptional support to our valued customers.

We've delved into the importance of aligning organizational goals with customer needs and expectations, understanding the significance of leading by example in fostering a customer-centric mindset among employees. Our discussions have emphasized the empowerment of employees to prioritize customer needs, whether it's through fostering empathy or providing training programs tailored to develop customer-centric skills.

Moreover, we've explored the integration of customer feedback into organizational processes, recognizing its role as a catalyst for continuous improvement. By analyzing feedback data, identifying trends, and incorporating insights into product development and service enhancements, we've seen how businesses can elevate the customer experience.

In addition, leveraging technology for multichannel support has emerged as a critical aspect of modern customer service. From implementing AI and machine learning technologies to optimizing support channels for mobile devices, we've witnessed the transformative power of technology in enhancing customer interactions.

Through it all, one overarching theme has emerged: the importance of exceptional customer support. It's not just about resolving issues; it's about building lasting relationships and earning the trust and loyalty of our customers.

As we wrap up our exploration, let's remember that customer support isn't just a department; it's a mindset that should permeate every aspect of our organization. By prioritizing customer needs and striving for excellence in every interaction, we can pave the way for long-term success and growth.

I can't stress enough the pivotal role of exceptional customer support in our business. It's not just about solving problems; it's about building relationships and earning the trust and loyalty of our customers.

When a customer reaches out to us with an issue or a question, they're putting their trust in our ability to help them. How we handle that interaction can make all the difference. By providing timely, helpful, and empathetic support, we're resolving their immediate concerns and showing them that we value their business and care about their experience.

And that's where the magic happens. When customers feel heard, understood, and well taken care of, they're more likely to stick around. They become loyal advocates for our brand, spreading positive word-of-mouth and driving growth through referrals.

However, it's not just about retaining existing customers; exceptional support also has a ripple effect on our brand reputation. Hearing about the great experiences others have had with us enhances our credibility and attracts new customers to our business.

So, as we move forward, let's remember the power of exceptional customer support. It's not just another department; it's the heartbeat of our business, driving trust, loyalty, and growth. By prioritizing the needs of our customers and delivering exceptional experiences every step of the way, we're not just meeting expectations; we're exceeding them. And that's what sets us apart in today's competitive landscape.

Customer support isn't just a box to tick; it should be right up there at the top of our priority list. Why? Because it's the backbone of our business, the lifeline that connects us to our customers.

Investing in customer support isn't just about buying fancy tools or hiring more staff. It's about recognizing the value of every interaction with our customers and ensuring we're equipped to handle them with care and efficiency.

That means ongoing investment in training our support teams, ensuring they have the skills and knowledge to tackle any challenge that comes their way. It means staying ahead of the curve regarding technology and leveraging the latest tools and platforms to streamline processes and enhance the customer experience.

Perhaps most importantly, it means recognizing that customer support isn't a one-time fix. It's a journey, an ongoing commitment to putting our customers first and continuously striving to improve their experience.

So, my fellow business owners, let's make a pledge today to prioritize customer support in everything we do. Let's invest the time, effort, and resources needed to ensure every interaction with our customers leaves them feeling valued, heard, and satisfied. Because, in the end, that's what will set us apart and drive our success in the long run.

As we wrap up our discussion, I want to emphasize the importance of embracing a continuous improvement culture in our customer support approach. It's not enough to just meet the bare minimum; we should always strive to do better, exceed expectations, and learn from every interaction.

To achieve this, we need to create an environment where feedback is not only welcomed but actively encouraged. That means reaching out to our customers and asking them for their thoughts and suggestions on how we can improve. It also means listening to our frontline employees, who often have valuable insights into our customers' challenges and opportunities.

However, soliciting feedback is only half the battle; we also need to take action on it. That means analyzing the feedback we receive, identifying common themes and areas for improvement, and then implementing changes based on that feedback. It might mean tweaking our processes, investing in additional training for our team, or even rethinking how we approach certain business aspects.

By committing to this cycle of feedback and improvement, we can ensure we're always evolving and adapting to meet our customers' changing needs and expectations. And ultimately, that's what will set us apart and keep our business thriving in the long run.

I want to take a moment to express my gratitude for the opportunity to dive into this important topic. Customer support isn't just about solving problems; it's about building relationships and creating positive experiences that keep customers coming back.

I hope our customer support exploration has provided you with valuable insights and strategies you can apply to your business. Remember, exceptional customer support isn't just a nice-to-have; it's essential for building trust, loyalty, and long-term success.

As you move forward, I encourage you to take action. Take what you've learned and put it into practice. Whether implementing new technologies, training your team, or simply committing to always putting your customers first, every step

MASTERING CUSTOMER SUPPORT

you take toward delivering exceptional customer support will pay off in the long run.

Thank you for joining me on this journey, and here's to creating memorable experiences for our customers and building stronger, more successful businesses together.

Work Less and Make More Money Than Ever Before

Take your business to the next level
with a fresh perspective.

Jason Miller's insights show you exactly how to break through plateaus and achieve big profits.

Go beyond your expectations and
see what's possible for your business.

jetlaunch.link/SABdiscover

About the Author

Jason Miller is an accomplished business leader with over thirty years of experience, renowned for his expertise in hyper company growth, scaling, and strategic and operational implementation. He founded the Strategic Advisor Board (SAB) in 2017 and served as its Senior Global Council Member, overseeing its global operations and team capabilities. In addition to his primary role at SAB, Jason holds multiple chair positions across various companies and nonprofits. He has built more than twenty-four companies from scratch since 2001 and is dedicated to crafting sustainable business models emphasizing leadership responsibility, strategy, and accountability.

Known for his no-excuses approach and nicknamed "The Bull," Jason has advised thousands of global leaders. He has been recognized as a foremost expert in consulting for creating scalable business models, particularly for small and mid-market companies. His focus extends to fostering a positive company culture, enhancing staff retention, and deepening customer loyalty, believing that a clear vision and purpose are essential for impactful business. As a veteran, Jason is committed to serving veteran-owned companies and provides pro bono services to veteran organizations as part of a five-year plan.

Jason holds an MBA from Trident University and credits the "school of hard knocks" for his doctorate in practical experience. He is affiliated with numerous prestigious organizations that impact business globally, such as the American Club Association, Leigh Steinberg Academy, Forbes Council, and Entrepreneur Magazine Leadership Council. A lifetime member of the American Legion, Disabled American Veterans, and Veterans of Foreign Wars, Jason lives in Boulder, Colorado, with his family. He focuses on professional development and business strategy to serve his clients better.